Resumes from Hell

Jon Reed and Rachel Meyers

Illustrations by Rusty Johnson

Published by eCruiting Alternatives, Inc.
Web site: www.resumesfromhell.com

Distribution by Ingram and Baker & Taylor

ISBN 0-9725988-1-2

Cover and interior design by Rusty Johnson
Title page logo design by Kyle and Chris Cross
Copy edit by Amy Theophile

Dedications

Jon Reed: *I'd like to dedicate this book to all my co-workers who worked with me from 1995-2000 as the resumes poured in. Your camaraderie made the great days better and the hard days dealable.*

Rachel Meyers: *I'd like to dedicate this book to my father, who taught me the importance of hard work, entrepreneurship, and keeping a "joke file."*

Acknowledgements

The authors would like to acknowledge the following people for their generous time in the development of this book for publication. Thanks goes out to Sarah Larson and Patrick Borelli for their vital support and encouragement during the early stages of this project. For his invaluable legal expertise, we are indebted to Zick Rubin. Others who have provided crucial assistance include: Paul Bissex, Amy Theophile, Joe Minton, Seth Spaulding, Ken Grey, and Jack Cameron. Thanks also to Kyle and Chris Cross for their logo contribution to www.resumesfromhell.com. And finally, a special thanks to Morris Rosenthal for his indispensable guidance regarding all aspects of the publishing process.

Disclaimer

About the Resume Excerpts in This Book (Yes, They're Real)

The resume excerpts in *Resumes from Hell* are based on selections from actual resumes that Jon and Rachel received while working as recruiters from 1995-2000. To protect the confidentiality and anonymity of all parties, names and other identifying details have been altered. All the names in this book are fictitious - any resemblance to individuals living or dead is coincidental. All addresses, phone numbers, and email addresses have been changed, as well as dates of employment and names of employers. Many employer names are fictitious. Some real company names were used, but never ones that the individual in question actually worked for.

Contents

Introduction

Why Are Bad Resumes Funny?
And Why Are Funny Resumes Bad?

We've all seen this phenomenon: after a certain point, bad things turn funny. Movies are the perfect example: some movies are just so "Gigli" that we can't stop laughing. Others even earn a cult following. But not so with the bad resume. A bad resume is more of a private phenomenon. Until now.

Laughing at a bad resume is like laughing at someone who slips and falls on the ice. It's funny only as long as they get back up. But as long as they're down, they do provide the rest of us with an entertaining dose of "how-not-to's" that we are well advised not-to-follow.

For the purposes of this book, a bad resume is simply a resume that does not achieve its fundamental purpose: to present the job seeker in a positive light compared to the competition. Funny resumes - this book's obsession - are bad resumes that fail this objective in unique and unusual ways. Instead of being littered with typos, a funny resume is usually tainted by one or two unfortunate gaffes that inspire the hiring manager to file it away in their "funny file."

To understand why some of these people fell, you have to know something about how hiring managers evaluate resumes and what they are (and aren't) looking for. As commission-based recruiters for ten years, your authors learned how managers feel about bad resumes the hard way: no hires, no food on table. This inside info helps to set the scene for the individual sections of this book, and might even provide a little help-on-the-fly for those readers who want to improve their resumes without poring over a bland "how to write a good resume" tutorial.

But why do funny resumes have to be bad? Isn't there such a thing as a "good" funny resume, a resume that entertains while at the same time enhancing the credibility and prospects of the job seeker? The "good" funny resume does indeed exist, but it's a rare phenomenon that's more of a miraculous accident than a sure-fire methodology to imitate. To prove their existence, at the end of this book, we do include a small section of resumes that entertained us without derailing the job seeker. But it's interesting to note that even these "good" funny resumes didn't really improve the job seekers' prospects. Their credentials were scrutinized just the same.

It's hard to make resumes funny *and* good because of the limitations of the medium. To be sure, there are certain industries where creative presentations are more effective (advertising, graphic design, and entertainment come to mind). But even in these fields, the "flava" is in the creative samples you might include along with (but not in place of) a traditional resume. Artists beware: resumes were never meant to be a satisfying form of self-expression.

The vast majority of our book's examples come from job searches we conducted in the Information Technology (IT) field. Although IT isn't the most conservative field we can think of, it's fair to say that most of our clients had a fairly corporate image, and resumes (and cover letters) were assessed with that in mind.

On the other hand, some of our most eyebrow-curling excerpts came from searches we did for computer gaming companies that, in theory, should be more open to hiring folks with a "wilder side." But as a general rule, the more fun the job seeker had with their resume, the less fun they had waiting for a call back. The resume writers you'll meet in the coming pages are, with a few glaring exceptions, competent professionals. But they assumed that the resumes they sent to us were the right vehicle for sharing off-the-beaten-track adventures, controversial opinions, and the occasional piece of titillating personal information.

Sooner or later, the skeptical among you are going to wonder: are the people in this book for real? Yes - all of the excerpts in this book are taken from actual resumes and cover letters we received from 1995 to 2000. Of course, to ensure the job seekers' anonymity, certain identifying details have been altered. But otherwise, these resume excerpts appear *as we received them* - typos and all. In a few instances, we removed typos that made the examples unreadable. So if you see a typo, our defense is that in this book, all typos are intentional. Any humorous consequences of said typos are, of course, also intentional. If only we could say that about all of our publishing projects!

Although the principles of resume badness transcend the IT field, you will notice that many of our examples do contain IT lingo and technical references. The good news is that you don't need to know the lingo to appreciate the humor. We can say that with confidence because we ourselves would fail a test that required us to define these terms in much detail. So while you don't need to understand IT terminology to enjoy this book, remember that when someone is applying for an IT job, hands-on experience is paramount. If they don't have the specific technical skills required, they have no shot at the position, regardless of how high they turn up the charm. And no, highlighting various certifications (especially failed ones) is not a good way to compensate for a lack of hands-on skills.

Finally, we would be remiss if we didn't acknowledge that the job market is serious business these days. Truly, we owe these "bad resume pioneers" a debt of gratitude for not only entertaining us, but for showing us what to avoid as we pursue our prospects in a job-scarce "global economy." As *The New York Times* noted in November of 2002, the average resume is rife with the kinds of mistakes that cause an inundated hiring manager to fire off their "thanks but no thanks" email templates. Given the imperfect competition, a good resume is an edge we can seriously use. As for the bad ones, they never really seem to get their due. It's about time.

1
Hobbies and Other Strange Pursuits

The job seeker's hobby is the hiring manager's future liability. When we think "skydiving," we think "exciting new adventure"; the potential employer thinks "high-risk outdoor activity." By adding leisure to our resumes, we hope to appear worldly and well-rounded, but here's the catch: you never know what's going to raise the corporate eyebrow. The rules of the game are as follows: we write the resume to get the job to get the paycheck to rent the plane, which we proceed to jump out of each weekend. Then we haul our sleep-deprived selves out of bed on Monday morning and do it all over again. The sticking point is that the hiring manager sees a lot of filing and collating in our future - tasks which are more readily performed by those with no social life, sports injuries, or distracting extracurricular activities. So we tone it down, reminding ourselves that our resumes are (fortunately) not our biographies. They don't have to tell the full story - that story is much more colorful and, for that matter, probably worthy of a book all its own. Here are some folks who should have saved their personal details for their autobiography.

• • •

When I'm not programming, I perform magic. I like solar applications, optical stuff, cool technology, and anything to do with radio waves. I juggle and twist balloon animals. I bungee jump on occasion, and I would like to experience skydiving soon.

As a Teach America volunteer, I teach troubled youth to build their own steam-powered bicycles.

• • •

• • •

I was also rather active in the ham-radio club of the school. As soon as I started studying I became one of the first members of this club after it had been without any members for two years in a row. Together with a few other freshman we blew new life into this club.

• • •

Memberships:
National Rifle Association
Trout Unlimited
Ducks Unlimited
Grouse Unlimited
Quail Unlimited
National Wild Turkey Federation

• • •

Activities:

My avocations include yacht deliveries (summer of '85 returned a 76 ft. yawl from latitude 56 in Canada to San Jose; a gaff-rigged schooner from San Francisco to Honolulu; a 68 ft. sloop from Los Angeles to Tahiti). At home I restore antique clocks, and old British violins. I campaign a wooden sloop and am an active volunteer at the Naval Museum doing machining and woodwork projects to restore and maintain the boats and ships.

• • •

Hobbies:
family, jogging, training mechanisms, reading, business

• • •

Interests
Herpetology, soccer coaching, music, virtual reality.

• • •

I am attending college to obtain two degrees and three certificates in the field of Computer Science.

In my spare time I like to work on my computer and do various activities with my girlfriend.

• • •

Interests: Rock climbing, Billiards, Canoeing, Didjeridu, Aikido, Vespas, Sanskrit, Geography & Travel, Linguistics & Literature, Culture & Cinema, Craniology, Arts & Opera, Theoretical Mathematics, Quantum Physics, Philosophy & Religion, Astronomy, Indian Headdresses, and Tribal Aboriginal Music.

• • •

2
TMI (Too Much Information)

When it comes to resumes, you don't have to say a lot to say too much. We call this phenomenon "Too Much Information," or "TMI." The phrase "TMI" is borrowed from other contexts, such as reality TV shows. We think we've seen it all, but then we have to watch somebody urinating on someone else's leg to soothe a jellyfish sting. That's "TMI." When you get a case of "TMI" on a resume or cover letter, invariably the job seeker has veered off course from providing work-related details in order to divulge personal and private information. There are some things an employer just doesn't need to know - at least until we secure a cubicle with our name on it.

• • •

This is so cool; learning more about the Internet is third on my wish list - right below July rent and being able to afford a decent haircut. I am computer literate, with experience in several word processing and spreadsheet applications. What I am doing now is temporary work, because I need the money. Astrology and Tarot readings are my specialties, because I like helping people gain insight into themselves and, frequently, a wider perspective on their problems. However, business has been very slow and I am looking for a steady source of income.

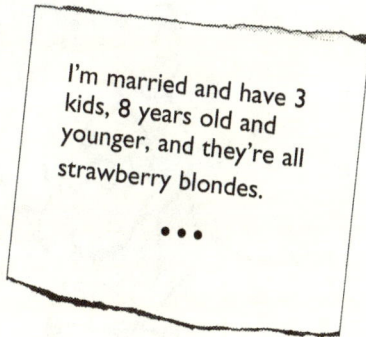

I'm married and have 3 kids, 8 years old and younger, and they're all strawberry blondes.

• • •

• • •

My domain name "TechPoetEng" is a reflection of my self-analysis: First a Technologist, Second a Poet, & Third an Engineer. Last day sick in 1985. No medications/no symptoms/no allergies. I take care of my body and take care of my mind.

• • •

Objectives:
To be a part of a team with an opportunity to learn and use skills acquired with a view for professional growth. My goal is the pursuit of excellence in my chosen field.

Strengths:
Good communication skills, able to work under pressure, ability to learn quickly.

Weakness:
Sentimental and starts crying fast.

• • •

Weakness: Sentimental and starts crying fast

Personal:
Dynamic and passionate about work and life. Consummate professional. Takes great pride in what he does. Born and raised in Chicago. (spent over 35 years there.) Very polished, smooth, quick on his feet. Makes a strong and commanding presence - tall (6'4", 235 pounds), athletic, sophisticated and mature. Engaging personality with quick wit, warm smile, happy demeanor, high energy level and enthusiasm. Effervescent and fun to be around. A leader. A late bloomer. Very communicative. Enjoys writing and public speaking. Excellent presenter. Happily married to a Norwegian beauty with two scrumptious children (Jeremy and Tina) ages 5 and 4 respectively.

Above is only an outline, would enjoy discussing/talking further unification: Able to work from home in the beginning at say about $150 per week to cover expenses and to help get the ball rolling! House is paid for, so I have junk food, shelter, stereo, equipment, resources, modem, and a bathroom!

• • •

• • •

My present emoluments are 115K plus incentive and bonus. I am married and very active in my personal life too.

• • •

Name:
Dr. Ravesh Bharatham

Date of birth:
July 23, 1972

Marital Status:
Un-married

Identification Marks:
1. A mole below the right shoulder near the neck.
2. A light mole on the chin at the left side.

• • •

First, I was born...

This gentleman's resume takes him back to before his birth:

1965 - 1969 Indiana State University School of Business

1951 - 1964 Kindergarten through high school in the Locksbury Central School system.

1946 December 18, Born, Binghamton, NY, to Elmer and Esther Williams.

1942 - 1948 Family lived in employee apartments at Wellington State Mental Hospital, where Mom worked as a ward attendant until I was born, and where Dad continued to work as a security officer.

• • •

The one thing I enjoy short of an orgasm would have to be creating things; using my mind to come up with new and unusual concepts and ideas that may or may not have been thought of before.

• • •

Married current spouse in September, 1974. Have 3 children, born

Jan, 1976	San Jose	Elora
June, 1982	San Jose	Jules
Feb, 1987	Sacramento	Sandy

Also have several animals = 4 dogs; 5 ferrets; 3 cats; many fish

• • •

We have received not one, but two complete residence histories during the course of our recruiting careers:

JIMMY J. MATTHEWS
3 Woodcreek Lane, Baltimore, MD - 21204
http://us.net/04565-resume
y4565@us.net

VITALS:

DOB	02/01/41
POB	Salt Lake City, Utah

Primary Residence	Dates:
Dallas, TX	1944 - 1948
Holland, MI.	1948 - 1950
Springfield, IL	1950 - 1960
Transient -	1961 -
Tallahassee, FL	1961 - 1962
International transient	1963 - 1965
Little Rock, AK	1965 - 1967
San Antonio, TX	1967 - 1969
Shreveport, LA	1970 - 1971
Sioux Falls, SD	1972 - 1974
Santa Clara, CA	1974 - 1976
Poughkeepsie, NY	1977 - 1978
Santa Clara, CA	1978 - 1980
Reno, NV	1980 - Present

Note: Have resided at current address since May, 1980 (stability?)

• • •

Residence History of Jim McDaniels
Revised May 1999

5-99 to Present	136 Lincoln Terrace, Ann Arbor, MI
5-95 to 5-99	Box 513, Preston, ID
6-91 to 5-95	Box 103, Franklin, ID
11-89 to 6-91	Box 343, Akron, OH
4-88 to 11-89	Box 15, Cleveland, OH
5-87 to 4-88	Box 37B, Shreveport, LA
6-86 to 5-87	Plot #8, Sea Island, FL
12-84 to 6-86	2315 15th St., Sarasota, FL
6-81 to 12-84	1902 36thAve., E. Bartlesville, OK
4-79 to 6-81	2408 6th St., S. Oklahoma City, OK
5-78 to 4-79	Box 47B, Richmond, KY
6-76 to 5-78	Lexington, KY
3-75 to 6-76	Clarkson, KY
5-70 to 3-75	White Plains, KY

• • •

My family have pretty much given up trying to understand how I make a living, although it broke my mother's heart that I should be so successful, and yet have no way to brag about it other than to say "Oh, he's in computers." My family still asks, now and then, mostly out of politeness, and I still work at a description. But there is a sort of pained smile, a sort of glazed expression to the eyes, that indicates that perhaps the listener isn't really as interested in atomized transfer functions as he first let on, and I have learned that it is simplest to say… When my boss comes into my office with a problem that needs to be solved, I solve that problem.

• • •

Since the project was coming to a close and it was obvious I was leaving anyway, after the last bugs were fixed, I was fired, and my credits in the game were all but removed to make it more difficult to get a job with a competitor. It's a given that Mike Stevenson, my old boss, has been calling up everyone in the industry spreading God only knows what types of hideous rumours about me, to scare off any competitors from hiring me.

• • •

Career Summary

Early in my career I realized that inter-departmental information flow was the "grit in the gears of industry." Beginning on the factory floor in the 70's, I pioneered what is now called TIP, or "technology integrated production", which allows the corporation's business information to push manufacturing instead of vice versa. In the 80's, I learned how to predict the interactions of an Integrated Network using computer simulation to avoid expensive mistakes in large scale implementations. In the 90's, at General Mills, I learned what big really means.

• • •

Personal:
1. A Scorpio born in the year of Ox, in Hong Kong; spiritually fit.
2. Seriously like non-popular music (including Peking Opera) and classic sports, especially tennis.

• • •

Here we have a special subsection of TMI: folks who get ahead of themselves on their resumes and cover letters. These people provide a level of job, salary, and benefits requirements that would be more appropriate in a second or third job interview:

Other Data for Christopher Grisanti

Recruiters take notice: Salary requirements are negotiable and dependant upon job duties, location, benefits package, and other considerations. To receive an accurate estimate of salary requirements, please provide me with as much information as possible. An example would be that of an engineering or management position in a metropolitan area, (except California), with excellent health/dental insurance, matching 401K plan up to 10% of salary. In this case my requirements would start at $70-80K annual for a max 45 hr week with relocation assistance. However, each situation is different, so proceed at your own risk.

• • •

What geographic preferences do you have?

To be specific, I am interested in an area that is not too urban - or at least which offers the ability to live outside heavily populated urban areas within a short commute - and one which offers recreational and social opportunities. I am a single heterosexual male, 32 years old, and while that has absolutely nothing to do with employment, I am seeking to relocate to an area which is more enjoyable to live in and not just work in. I enjoy the beach and it would be very nice to live within a couple hours of a coast; at the same time, I also enjoy the mountains. Once again, if a person is happier in their environment and with their life away from work, they are bound to be more productive AT work.

• • •

3
"Actually, I'm Not As Qualified As You Think I Am"

The "I'm Not Qualified" resume is the calling card of the person whose honesty you respect, but whose connection to the reality of the working world you question deeply. The "Not Qualified" resume writer is mysteriously compelled to make job and career-related confessions. They fill us in on projects that were never completed, degrees that were never awarded, and performance that was not up to snuff. They make passing references to bad test scores, point out their lack of accomplishments, and cross their fingers. Inexplicably, these "Not Qualified" types seem to play down their best skills, instead showcasing the most random and under-qualified aspects of their background. We can speculate on their motivations all we like, but the phenomena of the "I'm Not Qualified" resume persists despite all rational explanation.

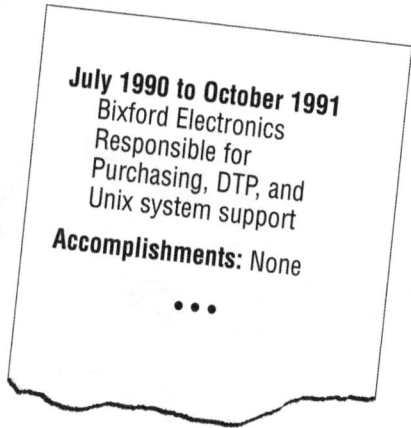

July 1990 to October 1991
Bixford Electronics
Responsible for
Purchasing, DTP, and
Unix system support

Accomplishments: None

• • •

• • •

1992-1996
Intellifax
Software Department Manager
Electronic exchange development, modem
communication project.
This work wasn't finished.

• • •

73% is passing; I scored 71%

Strengths: In the last sixteen months, I have devoted hundreds of hours to studying and programming in Visual Basic at home. On April 29, 1995, I took the VB 6.0 Advanced Concepts Exam, and was two correct answers shy of becoming a Certified Visual Basic Developer: 73% is passing; I scored 71%.

• • •

REMINDER...

Please Remember dear Sir/Madam,
That I have failed in a few subjects during my Diploma in
Computer Engineering, and that I have no Degree...

• • •

It is possible for me to run windows apps on my
machine if I buy the software, but that is not my
purpose! If all you are currently interested in is
doing/seeing/creating some beautiful images, they can
be saved or sent on zip cartridges and seen on both
platforms. I do not have any programming skills so
you know way better than I what is possible. Also, I
have one or two ideas for screenplays, but you are
not advertising for that.

• • •

Dear Jon,
Can you help me find an ERP job?

PROS:
Expert in my field (Access Database)
Get problems solved
Worked with very large databases

CONS:
No ERP practical experience
Not certified
Age

• • •

Last APL contract expired in November. To complete project was working 60 hour week. AT THE SAME TIME was doing Cobol course part-time from instructor who was teaching for the first time having just come off the course himself. Despite flunking the test, I feel I got 90%+ for the theoretical section and for completing two of the three coding exercises. I thought I did them well so was surprised not to be certified, but suspect that as one was dependent on another I did not even attempt, the completed one did not run and so may have been disqualified.

I'm worse off than ever before as APL is dying.

• • •

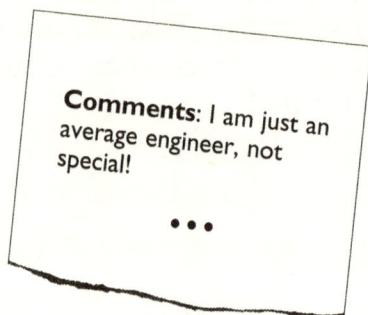

Comments: I am just an average engineer, not special!

• • •

4
Questionable References

Providing unsolicited references is a violation of the "don't ask, don't tell" policy of resume writing. On the surface, listing references might seem like a risk-free, straightforward chance to embellish our qualifications. But as you'll see below, we don't all define reference-giving in the same way. Whereas one person might list the names and numbers of a few former colleagues, another person might include their mother. When it comes to "Questionable References," the devil really is in the details.

• • •

This applicant manually typed his own "Notes" at the bottom of his letters of reference, where he elaborated on his relationship with the reference-givers:

NOTE: NOT PART OF THE ABOVE: Dr. Frank C. Peterson had a PhD in both Physics and Mathematics, and was a fantastic person to work with and play with (I suspect our play would be called work by others, but we enjoyed our work so well that when we did things for Science, for which we were not paid, we called it play and it really was for us.) I only wish he was still with us (RIP). Andrew L. Polanski

NOTE: NOT PART OF THE ABOVE: Tim Freeman knew nothing about Performance Testing, never did, but he got the job when I left for better fields (Caltron wouldn't make me the VP I wanted). He liked me and I hope he hired someone who could do the job, under him. Andrew L. Polanski

• • •

If you call my previous employer, they'll tell you that my technologies were also used in Bone Crunch Football and Master Blastoff (hook up your Caller ID blocker before calling this reference, these people are slime).

• • •

References:

Name:	Description:
Linda Bell	She was my Acquisitions Editor at McGraw-Hill.
Andy Wilkinson	I worked with his company briefly, supporting all of their telecomm devices and equipment.
Timothy Davis	Cousin. Past marketing and consulting client.
Dan Rosenthal	My older brother. We have been "besting" each other's technological accomplishments all our lives.
Jane Rosenthal	Mother. She's funded a lot of my research.

• • •

This applicant had trouble following his own instructions:

Kindly provide three Technical References (peer level):

1) Mark Peabody 47 Locust Drive, Austin, TX 78701
2) George Marshall 685 Hill Crest Drive, San Diego, CA 92106
3) Larry Richter 543 Washington Blvd., Wilmington, DE, 19808
4) Harry Spencer 564 Orchard Lane, Wilmington, DE 19803
5) Kevin Ellsworth 24 Seaside Terrace, Lauderdale, Florida 33355

• • •

Dear Sirs,
Why would you want to hire Juan Santos?

Perhaps we could meet and I could give you the names of 50 or 100 people at my previous positions who would be glad to give me a reference.

• • •

5
Problematic Public Personas

The question is raised: why would someone put a vanity email address on their resume, or an overly personal tag line on their correspondence? Whatever the reason, the folks below opted not to create a separate email address for job search correspondence. Maybe we all need to ask ourselves why there's so little time to create a professional online identity, but so much time to watch "American Idol." True, it's a whole lot easier to spend a summer catching up on "ER" reruns when you don't have a job; Rachel can attest to that. But it's hard to score a job as a medical assistant with rachelluvsER@tvcomesfirst.com on your resume.

• • •

Please consider my attached resume.

Bigger Faster Better More

    r i c k y

• • •

Greetings Mr. Reed,

I am ArchiTecture, a composer/audio designer who offers services in the multimedia field. Being classically trained with a BA in Music Education gives me the edge of being able to create music of most genres. May I ship a techno/electronic based CD demo to your company's Sound Producer?

Thank you for your precious time.

Sincerely,

ArchiTecture

• • •

These resume email addresses raised a few eyebrows around our office:

Pranav Gupta, kissme@unstoppable.com

Dan Simpson, pizza@tastyliving.com

David S., daaaaave@weirddudes.com

• • •

The following three email "signatures" caught our eye:

I would like you to reconsider my resume and application for the jobs I indicated. I have been out of school for three years now and have been working in a computer related field. I believe this qualifies me for your consideration.
Thank you,
-RICK

And if you look in me
afraid to see
you might find dreams of
insanity
but think again
my friend
resist the voices
you may hear
inside you'll find
no need to fear
my lunacy

• • •

Very truly yours,

Wilson G. Simmons

• • •

Hello!

I would like you to consider me for Oracle DBA jobs or any other similar opening befitting my experience and skills. For any further queries you can either email me or phone me up here in Melbourne.
Thank you.
Regards,
Suni

Banshee Boy from the land of Beer, Beaches, Barbeque, and Babes

---

• • •

6
Careful with That "Send" Button: Know Your Technology

Quick quiz: what's the most dangerous button on your email program? How many of you said "reply to all"? It's bad enough to send the Klez virus to everyone in your address book, but what happens when you follow up the perfect resume with the perfectly embarrassing email? Where the hell is the UNSEND button? The folks in this category did not have the benefit of such advanced technology, and as a result, they made gaffes and bloopers which have stood the test of time. The kicker question: do these types of mistakes hamper your chances with a prospective employer? Sometimes they do, sometimes they don't. But one thing cannot be denied: their entertainment value.

• • •

This was this job seeker's entire email:

I

• • •

Hi Jon - it's been a little while since we talked. I ended up over at Johnson and Johnson in a full time position. I saw a position in this week's newsletter that I'm interested in. It may be a stretch but, I thought I'd drop you a line with my latest resume and see what you think. Hope all is well.

Gdog G Gdog

This email was accidentally sent to our recruiting agency by someone intending to email a friend:

Keep me posted on which headhunters you deal with. I am currently tied into 50-70 placement agencies, none of which are aware of the others.

• • •

(At first, we wondered if this job-seeker was trying out his new hip-hop nickname, "Gdog." But it was actually his "Guard Dog" security program gone berserk, replacing his name and contact information with Gdog gibberish.)

• • •

These three job seekers had trouble with their resume templates:

Experience

07/94 - Present: Permacare, Portland, Oregon
      Lab assistant. Provided? Prepared? Assisted? … Use Action
Verbs.

• • •

Rita P. Gilmore

OBJECTIVE
_____

[Type Objective Here]

WORK EXPERIENCE
_____

      19xx - 19xx   [Company/Institution Name]   [City, State]
      [Job Title]
            • [Details of position, award, or achievement.]

WORK EXPERIENCE
_____

      19xx - 19xx   [Company/Institution Name]   [City, State]
      [Job Title]
            • [Details of position, award, or achievement.]

WORK EXPERIENCE
_____

      19xx - 19xx   [Company/Institution Name]   [City, State]
      [Job Title]
            • [Details of position, award, or achievement.]

VOLUNTEER EXPERIENCE
_____

[Click here and enter information.]

COMMUNITY ACTIVITIES
_____

[Click here and enter information.]

2308 WILDWOOD DRIVE _ JACKSONVILLE, FL 32209 _
RITAK@USMAIL.COM
(W) FAX (813)555-4550 (H)(813)555-6336

• • •

Alberto Vincenzo

Table of Contents

- <#accomp>Summary of Major Accomplishments and Current Focus

- <#History>Employment History

March 1980 - Present
Corporate Source International, Albany, NY 12204
  - <#pdarchitect>Product Development Architect
  - <#Architect> Senior Enterprise Architect
  - <#Special> Special Assignment
  - <#dir_MIS> Director of MIS
  - <#mgr_sysdev> Manager of Systems Development
  - <#proj_ldr> Project Leader
  - <#PA> Programmer/Analyst

<#education> Education - Training
<#interests> Other Interests
<#References> References

• • •

We remain fascinated by this surreal email we received from a sleepy job seeker:

I am very, very tired today, a particular kind of tired that I don't feel too often. I was sleeping on the couch, and I swore Tomi came home and was playing "Fortunate Son" on a steel-string acoustic guitar, but we don't have one of those, so I kept trying to force my eyes open to see and confirm his presence. I think the phone rang and I think it was a technical recruiter, but I really am not sure. I think I talked to him, and at some point I remember something like this:

He said, "[blah blah blah] the GUI properties dialog."

"Oh, yes, the GUI properties dialog."

"You don't know which one it is. You're just saying that to impress me."

I was silent, because I was actually asleep.

But I don't know if this conversation occurred or if I just made it up in the dream!

• • •

This personal email was meant for a friend, but was sent to a hiring manager by accident:

I had a message on my machine from you that said to call.

Got my new Business Week mags today. No new ads to mention. What did you do to get the phone ringing so much?

Sorry I was a crabby bitch today. God… what an awful day. After I talked to you I did the fall marketing brief on powerpoint for Sandy and saved it on a diskette. The diskette was bad or something and I had to do the whole thing over again. One-baaaaad-day.

Went to see Big Fat Greek Wedding tonight. It was hilarious. You'd like it. Anyway if you and SO (Cindy?…. right?) are looking for something to do it's a good one.

Have a good weekend. I'm going to the office for a couple hours in the am to get my shit together.

See ya,

Jane

Sorry I was a crabby bitch today

Another accidental email:

Hi Ted,

Yeah I saw that crap yesterday, I couldn't work out if the guy was joking or just delusional! Thanks for the custard recipe, I think it uses castor sugar, do you know what they call it over here? Jaihar is going to get his grandmother to try and make it.

We got the results back from her latest blood test and they are encouraging. The week before last the number was 43, last week was 67!!?? And this week was 36. Thank god the number had gone down. We would be *very* worried if it had gone up.

Regards,

Sanjay

P.S. Say hi to Sam and the dog for us.

• • •

This job seeker sent us a resume and then shortly thereafter sent along a strange message. Our best guess is that he was trying to post to a discussion group and had us on his list:

To All,

Can we get rid of this nonsense, bullshit warning message, it was around already a year ago. It surprises me that the content is not changed at all. What nonsense. Whoever came up with solid proof of real damage done by this virus, which makes a CPU a merry go round, stand up and get a beer and alka seltzer.

• • •

This job seeker demonstrates that even if your resume looks fine on your own computer, it might not look the same on other machines:

Claude Marcel

15 Fairway Drive Alternate Address

Cincinnati, OH, 45246　　**42 Franklin Avenue**

　　　　　Cleveland, OH, 44111

claude@netminder.com　**216 555 5486**

OBJECTIVE

I am preferably seeking employment that can be performed from home through telecommuting.

TECHNICAL SUMMARY

Hardware:	Experience Level:	Years:	Last Used:
Computers	Very Heavy	12 or more	2000
Scanners	Very Heavy	8 to 10	1998
Printers	Very Heavy	5 to 7	2000
Fax machines	Heavy	5 to 7	1999
Copiers	Light	8 to 10	1998
		2000	

Software:	Experience Level:	Years:	Last Used:
MS Office 95,97,2000	Very Heavy	5 to 7	2000
Corel WordPerfect suite	Heavy	3 to 4	1998
Dbase I,II,III,IV	Medium	1 to 2	1999
Microsoft Word, Excel, Access	Heavy	4 to 8	2000

Microsoft Power Point	Medium	5 to 7	2000
Microsoft Front Page	Very Heavy	4 to 7	1999
Microsoft Works	Medium	5 to 7	2000
Microsoft Publisher	Very Heavy	2 to 3	2000

Graphic: Used:	Experience Level:	Years:	Last
Microsoft Image Composor	Very Heavy	5 to 7	2000
Paint Shop Pro	Medium	3 to 4	2000
Adobe Illustrator	Light	1 to 2	2000
Poser	Light	1 to 2	2000
Adobe Photoshop	Light	1 to 2	2000
Microsoft Publisher	Light	1 to 2	2000

Experience Level:	Experience Level:	Years:	Last Used:
C++	Light	Less than 1	2000
Visual Basic	Light	Less than 1	2000
Cobol	Education Only	1 to 2	1985
Unix	Education Only	1 to 2	1985
Fortran	Light	Education Only 1 to 2	1984

• • •

This individual was trying to reconnect with an old friend who had posted to a technical discussion group. But instead of sending a private email, he sent an email to the entire group. There were a number of prominent recruiters and hiring managers on the list; let's hope his manager wasn't one of them:

Dave -

How's it going? Thought you'd be interested to know that I'm leaving Proctor and Gamble and just gave my notice (this isn't public yet). I asked the project manager when he thought the project wouldn't suffer timing-wise, and he said in February, so I'm going to be a lame duck for a while, but made it clear to him my first priority in December and January is the LSAT. I am still hoping to go to school next September, and will crash with Amber in the meantime (she says 'hello'). I pasted a letter I am sending to the on-line headhunters, I'd be interested in your thoughts if you have the time. Hope things are going well for you, and hope to hear from you...

• • •

We used to have an AOL email address that began with "nat," an abbreviation for "national," as in "national recruiting." That's the only explanation we have for this "case of mistaken identity" email we received one day from another AOL user:

Nat,

Just thought that I would drop you a line to see how you were doing...

Tanya is coming out to see me on my birthday (18th) for a few days, so it should be fun. She will probably want to go to clubs and meet guys, so I'm not sure how much of my time will be spent protecting her from the guidos and salvatores of this city. Other than that, I am going to try to get tickets to "Jenny Jones"; if I do, I'll let you know so you can tape our episode. I'm only trying to get us guest tickets, not actually appearing on stage, in case you were confused.

P H I L

P.S. What was your boyfriend's name again? I want to run his name thru the FBI security system and make sure he's not into any funny business.

• • •

7
Yeah, But How Do You Really Feel?

"Yeah, But How Do You Really Feel?" resume writers have a love/hate dynamic going with their employers, and they want to tell us about both sides of the relationship: "I liked my work, but hated my boss/company/project/co-workers/cubicle/parking space." These folks are onto the corporate games that people play. The problem is that job seeking is also a game, and the winners are rarely people with chips on their shoulders.

• • •

This is from an applicant's self-made questionnaire:

Would you consider contract work?
No - Have been used and abused too much using these vehicles.

• • •

I need a position offering more growth. Working for a government agency, there is a degree of "the way things are done" rather than "the best way to do things" or even "the most innovative new way of doing something." To stay at the same level of expertise to me is to go backwards with the way technology is advancing.

Additionally, it is because of my below scale compensation and a poor social environment that I am "looking around."

• • •

Things were great on the programming side, but on the company politics side, things were going to hell fast. The President of TrueVisionWare, Burt Nehlseen, is one of those psychotic high school bullies that enjoy torturing small animals. He would walk the halls of TrueVisionWare gloating about how he had screwed over his old employers, gloating about how he had screwed over his old co-workers, gloating about how he had screwed over some TVW employees last week, and gloating about how he was going to screw over some more TVW employees at next week's meeting. A real sweet guy. His favorite pastime is to call up his competitors and spread rumors, thus screwing over people he has never even met.

• • •

The reasons I'm seeking employment are listed below:

First, in the first Two-Weeks of November I worked 172 hrs and have yet to be compensated Overtime or Bonus.

Secondly, somewhere along the way (about the time my VP left and another came along) I lost control over "My" Schedule and Time. Thus, I've missed several of my Kids Xmas events.

About 4 mos ago, the Boss hired 30+ Sales people. He missed his revenue goal for the year and thus, the Board of Directors "Thumped" him. He made some significant "Changes" in the Org Structure (i.e., fired 50+ Sales people) Almost all other Biz Units Did Not reach their numbers this year. Proudly, mine did!

Most other VP's are close to retiring, therefore, they cannot Afford to Leave. Conversely, I have a couple of Rolls left in me. (If the Need Arises).

• • •

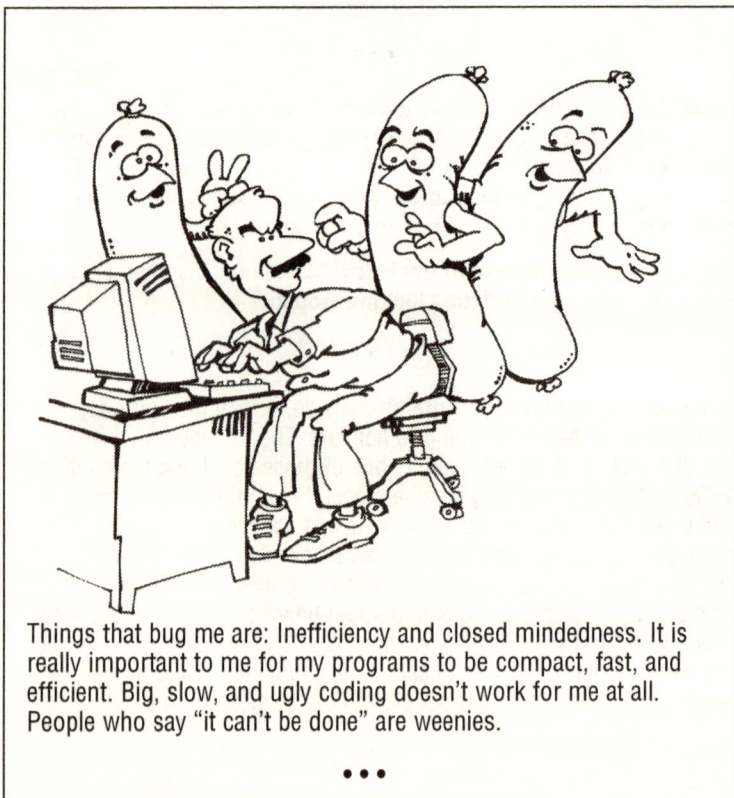

Things that bug me are: Inefficiency and closed mindedness. It is really important to me for my programs to be compact, fast, and efficient. Big, slow, and ugly coding doesn't work for me at all. People who say "it can't be done" are weenies.

• • •

8
Blown Away By My Own Abilities

During a job search, you are in charge of selling your product: you. That's why we think it's a great idea to be your own cheerleader. But the folks in this section took it one step further: they brought the whole marching band.

• • •

I am a "Nordstrom" rather than a "KMart." I am gifted with superior intellect, field independence and critical thinking. I am evenly introvert-extrovert, intuitive, feeling and perceptive. I am warmly enthusiastic, high-spirited, spontaneous, gently, ordinary, ingenious, imaginative and able to improvise. I'm quick with real solutions and ready to help others. I easily deal with the unexpected and quickly see things to be done. I believe goals, plans and organization reduce the need for work pressure; however, I enjoy the challenge of an unpreventable emergency that makes me work against time. Being and acting a worthy "Nordstrom," I am comfortable with both common and eminent people and situations.

• • •

83-86 Toyota: Authored Self-Correcting Automated QA/QC System. Went directly to each group/function and studied their operation, documented it, reviewed it with the people and modified A/R. Coordinated effort through Customer Interface. Specifically, I sold my system to both Toyota & US Gov. and got the plant shipping product, again. Worked 15-16 hr days, liked the people there and I got Sundays off. I was the guest of honor at the local Country Club to celebrate my success and their survival.

• • •

OBJECTIVE:
My objective is simple: I want your job. I don't mean the one I'm applying for, but *your* job.

I'm a communications major with a minor in creative writing at a California school. I still have 2 semesters to go, but I know more than some of my teachers. Once I hit the real world though, you're gonna hear from me.

• • •

Nesson International
Research Scientist (1973 - 1977)

Fresh out of school and out to change the world... A professor had warned me that I would be a "speeding bullet into a barrel of molasses". But, I did two important things before realizing that I didn't want to be a researcher. I revolutionized the retro reflective sheeting (highway sign) industry with a unique alternate reflector process that used the newest ultra-shine composite which quadrupled the product lifetime and doubled its performance. The other major accomplishment was recognizing the major health risks effecting workers and coordinating the firm's policy to enforce safety in the workplace. I am sure I saved lives.

• • •

I possess extraordinary communication, organization, management, marketing and strategic planning skills to be maximized. I am a true self starter who thrives on challenge and vision. I savor interfacing with all people as part of my gregarious nature via any medium or vis a vis. There is no question I will be a major attribute for the right firm. Please speak with me at your earliest convenience.

• • •

I looked at the "proven Automated Graphic Maker code" and just shook my head. Sad, really sad. The approach and tradeoffs the code made were all the wrong ones to make, there basically was not a function I could not double the speed. One of the first things I did was to throw the to-do list out the window and replace it with the AGM wish list, plus a few things that weren't even on the wish list because they were clearly impossible, like a self-populating root directory. I pulled off so many coding miracles that a bunch of my enhancements were sandbagged for next year's AGM.

• • •

Current Title: TV MOGUL / Famous TV & Movie Producer
• I am listed in the Official Marquis Who's Who in America

• I am a multi-millionaire TV & movie producer and software programmer

• I am listed in the Official Marquis Who's Who in America and Who's Who in Advertising

• I am a senior programmer / analyst in Visual Basic, Visual C++, Java

• • •

TARGET JOB
Desired Job: Employee
Desired Status: Full-Time
Salary: $15,000 a year

Description of my Perfect
Job: The richest woman in
the world. Author, public
announcer, genius.

• • •

Howdy,

My primary selling points are threefold: 1) I am competent technologically; 2) despite the former, I can still speak with normal humans, and they even tend to like working with me and for me; and 3) flying in the face of all reason, I also have artistic ability and my skills in various mediums allow me to incorporate pleasing content for the now media heavy web and applications market.

• • •

ORIGINATED

* Both World Level TCDs (2 decimal improvement for FCN, over the D-Receptor SLV) (My gift)

* 1st. Rechargeable Battery, Concept thru Lab. Work-up & Symposium W/TechWorld Co. to Publicize (My gift)

* 1st. Production Control Concept for Near-Critical-Mass Exception Handling (My gift)

* 1st in lots of less important things.

• • •

My exceptional creativity and problem solving ability has been officially validated at the top 2% of all college graduates applying to U.S. graduate schools.

• • •

I wrote, produced, and directed over 250 Successful Infomercials that featured over 250 Famous Celebrities. I wrote over 500 of the world's most famous and successful Direct Mail Pieces.

• • •

I am both a superior technician and a superior director.
I am very comfortable in one-on-one situations,
interested in people, do things to make the other
conversation party relaxed, and work steadily and
patiently. Additionally, I am amiable, easy going,
relaxed, outgoing, persuasive, hospitable and broadly
knowledgeable.

• • •

I have a depth of experience that transcends products by way of
technical architectures and a wealth of practical, successful
implementations, along with the savvy to immediately adapt,
like a chameleon, to my surroundings.

• • •

Personal Attributes:

High I.Q. (member of MENSA.)

Flexible

**Enjoy a challenge. (I have accomplished a number of
things which the resident gurus thought impossible.)**

• • •

Some of my strengths are: I am really creative. I can
always find a way to do what needs to be done within
the parameters of what is available. People really like
me because I like people. I am really easy to work
with, and allow people to be however and whatever
they choose to be. I expect complete honesty and I
keep my relationships on an honest level at all costs.

• • •

Some people's accomplishments are best described in the third person as the next two examples demonstrate:

Mr. Fournier can setup a seal team type, a small but elite group that will create a Business Intelligence Infrastructure that pushes information.

Past Accomplishments:

(Due to possible legal issues and the broadcast nature of this document, the names of the clients are withheld.)

Retail: A $4.5 billion retail chain lost its fast rise 2 years ago. The management waited for a year doing traditional Chinese fire drill and finally in a panic called Mr. Reynolds to help out.

Telecommunications: The cellular division was getting clobbered by Sprint and MCI. Mr. Reynolds designed a marketing database scheme to stop the bleeding. Last time we heard, the architecture has been embraced and expanded.

Aerospace: Mr. Reynolds was responsible in the supervision of the design of a self-guided space capsule. After the consulting firm of record failed to find a solution to eliminate a Challenger type disaster, Mr. Reynolds came up with the solution.

• • •

Dear Sir/Madam,

I know your company wants only the best and brightest ones. How about a guy who entered college at age of 14, graduated at age of 18, and will get his MS in Computer science at age of 20?

If that is not enough, what if this guy has an IQ > 150, won numerous awards, and is always considered by others as the smartest and the most hard-working ever seen?

Yes, this guy is me. I am the BEST available.

Below is my resume.

Chun Lee

• • •

As always, I still walk on water and bill at obscene rates. I charged SysWorks IT $178/hour plus expenses 3 years ago. I try to get in about 1,500 billing hours per year, so do the math accordingly.

• • •

I have nearly fifteen years of sales management and marketing experience - most of it with telecomm firms I either founded or moved rapidly into senior level management with. I have a rather unique background and skill-set. As a non-practicing lawyer, I can give significant legal advice, and work well with outside counsel.

Resume: I will hand-carry a resume to your office.

• • •

Today's businesses are just learning what I have known for years: data is useless unless it can be converted into information quickly and disseminated to all responsible parties in the decision chain. Change requires decisions. Decisions require information. Information requires business intelligence and integrated networks. That's what I do.

• • •

OBJECTIVE: In my previous work experience, I have done nothing but amaze my employers every step of the way, and I look to do the same, while gaining even more experience in the computer software industry.

• • •

They were going to hire me to run Make-to-Order if they got the Production Contract, which we did. But they didn't hire me and they spent a fortune in penalties. Served them right. They didn't know how to save money without getting in trouble, but I did. Oh well!

• • •

9
Computer-Philes for the Circular File

The feel-good message of the "Computer-Phile" is a simple one: with technology, "dreaming is our only barrier." But the dream of a new job might remain a dream unless the "Computer-Phile" can demonstrate that they are as interested in getting along with their co-workers as they are with their computers.

• • •

To be honest, I am a "technical" dude. As long as I talk with "techies" AND/OR "Trekkies", things are fine. When I am not, well lets just say that 9 years of intensive programming tend to transform your perception into black and white rather than the colorful hue most people are used to. I am (unfortunately) more of a "geek-speak" than a "chit-chat."

• • •

Additional Comments: MIS, Network, or Tech Support Management positions for small companies that are high tech in focus and have intensive network demands. Macintosh or Graphic Arts environments are special. Cross platform and complex networks are fun. If you don't have an Internet router, you're not alive.

• • •

... the Internet is already creating Magic by culminating this 'Simple but Infinite' Logical energy for 'Infinite processes'...

• • •

I manage the home network for my family. My sons (ages 9 and 14) each have a Macintosh LC in their bedroom, and are connected via Ethernet to the computer room where my wife and I work.

• • •

WE CAN DO ANYTHING IN PROGRAMMING BECAUSE WE HAVE THE BASIC & FUNDAMENTAL LOGIC - 'AND' 'OR' & 'NOT' IN OUR CONTROL, WITH WHICH ANY KIND OF INTELLIGENT LOGIC CAN BE BUILT. DREAMING IS OUR ONLY BARRIER.

What I Know right now is that EVERY DREAM CAN BE FULFILLED WITH PROGRAMMING, BECAUSE WE HAVE THE 'BASIC' AND THE 'FUNDAMENTAL LOGICAL SECRETS' IN OUR CONTROL: THE 'AND' LOGIC, THE 'OR' LOGIC AND THE 'NOT' LOGIC BORN WITH THE SIMPLEST AND THE BASIC EXISTENCE - THE DUAL 0 & 1 ! (upon which everything is built...)

WITH THESE BASIC LOGICS ALMOST ANY INTELLIGENCE IS POSSIBLE, ANY OUTPUT CAN BE ACHIEVED ! 10,000 % GUARANTEED !

• • •

Dear potential associate,

I have worked in the IS field for about 9 years now. If I were posed the question "how would you describe yourself," the answer would be, "I'm a self-motivated individual who responds with assertiveness and sincerity to INFO/SYS related issues."

• • •

Additional comments: I love computers. I have been behind
one for the past 10 years.

• • •

The Internet explosion should cause a radical
paradigm shift in how businesses operate, who they
view as their customers, and what they see as their
services and marketplace. In essence - the web
changes everything!

• • •

> **I love UNIX/LINUX and prefer it over Windows. I love networks. I love hardware. I am a non-smoker. I would love a testing position. I will be getting more into Perl and CGI soon. I would love to C++ test.**
>
> • • •

I like to code in C, C++, Fortran, Cobol, Pascal, and sometimes in Assembly. Recent years I am using Java. I am good at GUI and relational databases. I am able to program in Powerbuilder, dBase and Access. Frankly, I am a computer maniac. I do anything related to computers.

• • •

Creation comes in many forms, from babies, from words, to sounds, to images, etc., etc. The greatest thing about technology today is the ability to combine all these forms of creativity together. So where do all these forms of creativity merge to form an enterprise that is profitable? The video game industry! Multi-dimensional capitalistic art at its finest!

• • •

I am currently seeking a position in the competitive, enthusiastic world of The Computer Industry.

• • •

Of course, a CD project or even marketing a bibliography can be profitable, but what you are advertising for is a humanoid with advanced skills and very high creativity. Not all that easy to find AND acquire! I have been in touch with some Silicon Valley game nuts as well as companies on the net, and most say the problems they are encountering are not the game or programming, but the PUZZLES!

• • •

This thirty-something traced his computer experience all the way back to those early Radio Shack machines:

Early accomplishments:

Graphical demo: 10-minute-long compilation of original, mathematics-based, artistic renderings, morphs, and animations of the 5 letters: T-A-N-D-Y. Age 14

• • •

Hardware as you know is based on CPU and RAM and maybe a few goodies inside to make the machine "more better!" I just recently sold my 300 Mhz machine to purchase the hottest multiprocessor on the market! The machine is about $40,000 and MP apps will be between $1500 up to $15,000 EACH! Sorry, but Pentium chips are super strong but limited; but RISC based chips are far more flexible and can be aligned like military soldiers for unreal processing power!

• • •

Interests & Activities

"& bull; All of my activities are computer related"

• • •

10

Cover Letters: Generally Bad, Weird

If the resume is a slingshot, the cover letter is a hand grenade.
When a cover letter starts reading like a journal entry or an
excerpt from *Angela's Ashes,* the hiring manager simply sets it
aside and returns to it later, full of car wreck curiosity. In
theory, personalizing the cover letter with unconventional
touches seems like a great way to break down barriers
between hiring authority and job seeker. But the folks below
aren't achieving a new level of intimacy; they're setting off a
flare gun. They see the fireworks of self-expression; the
hiring manager sees a distress signal.

• • •

To,

The Technology Portfolio Planner,

It was at the age of 21, working with Bill Gates' baby
"RIGHTWORKS," and while still learning to deliver a networked
software environment, I was given the RESPONSIBILITY of project
management during a global QA certification audit, and

There were WINNERS and smiles.

Next CHALLENGE was at RS Software, where the thought of
switching to object technology and client-server computing
seemed monumental, but REUSE is REALITY today.

What NEXT?

To harness the power of XML and the Internet.

I have a DREAM to realize and

I know learning is an endless, endless journey.

You company is sure to find a SOLUTION in me.

• • •

You will inevitably ask yourself the question, "Why should I hire Terrence Jones rather than someone else?"

Your business requires a matrix of professional talent. The depth and variety of my experience as project manager is available ASAP to build business solutions for your company and its customers. "Success has 1,000 fathers. Failure is an orphan." Let me acknowledge a few of my legitimate offspring.

• • •

Right now, I am in Deputation at Applied Materials, for creating Displays.

Most of the time I end up in programming for some Engineering Activities, but nobody knows of it.

I shall put a strict full stop to all the temptation.

I have enclosed the detailed resume for your kind reference.

With Hope & Trust,

Thanking you,

Yours Sincerely,

M. E. Sapna Natarajan

• • •

Can you see a young man with successful PeopleSoft implementation experience? A young man with a thorough understanding of overall business operation? A young man who has excelled because of his extraordinary learning capabilities? I am that young man.

I would like to put my knowledge, experience and dedication to work for you. May I have an interview at your convenience? See that young man!

• • •

I would ideally
like to be placed
away from
the North Pole

Dear Mr. Reed,

My name is Shankar Venkatta.

I am looking for an opening as an Oracle professional in the United States or Canada.

I would like to get a job position as an Oracle professional with any moderately large Oracle consulting firm that have their own clients. This would give me multifunctional role in my job and therefore reduce the chance of monotony.

I do not have a specific preference for any industry but would like to avoid any high life risk industries.

I would ideally like to be placed in suburban Toronto or any English speaking part of Canada away from the north pole.

• • •

To,

THE COMPANY

WITH THE GOAL

FOR THE WORLD,

I am basically involved in 'programming' for about 11 years since childhood, but without a proper base.

I am already 27 now, and in vain to express myself fully. With 4 years of experience in an Engineering Consultancy.

Right now, I have no "proof" of any Degree, but this brief piece of text & the enclosed resume.

In my younger days, I spent my time searching for the truth behind the Digital binary secrets... "0, 1, And, Or, Not"... ending up with a deep knowledge of binary but 'not a wide' knowledge of other subjects. Unfortunately I could not cover the wide stories of other subjects; instead I spent 'full time' searching for the truth behind binary code, and risked my life in 'failing' in other subjects, during my quest for a 'Diploma in Engineering'. I understand that this will be the Biggest Barrier between you & me...

• • •

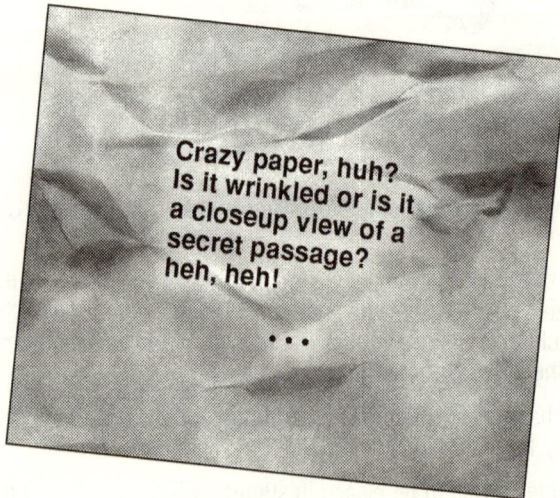

Crazy paper, huh? Is it wrinkled or is it a closeup view of a secret passage? heh, heh!

• • •

Dear invisible hiring hand of the video game industry,

America is a wonderful place to live, no? We're given the opportunity to follow virtually any desire we please, as long as we're willing to work hard and respect other people's happiness. It's no wonder half of the world either hates us, or wants to be just like us. My motto is "capitalism is for the chosen few." Of course, living in a capitalistic society, if we want to fulfill those desires and freedoms that have been so embedded into our minds as budding consumers, we must have the one thing our country is truly built upon... money. This means that for the majority of your life, you will have to be working for that money, so you can fulfill your desires. It's a nasty cycle, no?

• • •

HELLOOOOO, CYBERSLEUTHES!!!!!!!!

I have been looking for a company like yours for over a year! When I saw your job listing, things suddenly became VERY INTERESTING! The job you offer seems to be right down my alley! I have about 6 ga-zillion questions to ask you, but this is only "First Contact," so I guess I should proceed with the standard resume stuff first.

• • •

Dear Future Employer,

It is with great respect and awe that I write this letter.

I am a thirty-something year old woman... who is finished raising children and looking to join a dynamic company where I may utilize my computer/software/platform experience.

Skills which could be of immediate benefit to a client of yours in a creative industry would include:

* Writing. A creative mind combined with literary talent and a flair for writing, I have a limitless flow of fresh ideas on how to impact an audience.

* Editing. A Magna Cum Laude Bachelor of Arts in English with a bard's eye view on mending, bending, and transcending the habitual, the typical, and the traditional.

• • •

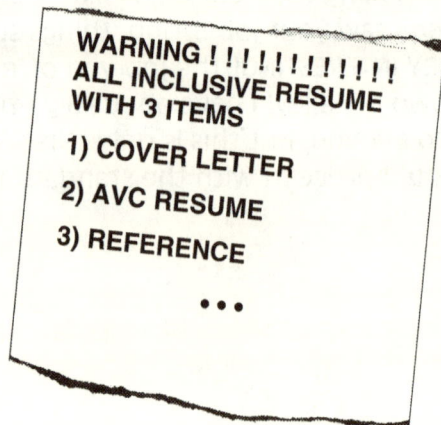

WARNING ! ! ! ! ! ! ! ! ! ! !
ALL INCLUSIVE RESUME
WITH 3 ITEMS

1) COVER LETTER

2) AVC RESUME

3) REFERENCE

• • •

A Perfect Holiday to any IT Professional (Be it a Recruiter, Manager - Channel Sales, Contractor, Vendor of IT services or any diversified roles that We or our Firm, may operate as) is only when his or her Job is perfectly done to the appreciation of the World around and becomes useful to the said End users.

In a bid not to fail in my job I need your cooperation all the time. And now, It is again your help I need to get the complete mailing address of your firm, if it is not too inconvenient to your goodselves. May I therefore request you to please email me the requested particulars.

I sincerely appreciate the cooperation and assure you that this is only for improving our relationship. Inconvenience, if any, is sincerely regretted. I await the receipt of your information.

Many Thanks

Sincerely

Stanley

(All this banter just to get our mailing address, which was readily available on our web site.)

● ● ●

If I were to wait for anything, I'd be waiting a long time. I create what I want, make it happen, and enjoy the learning process along the way.

What I believe is: When I make a difference in my relationships, I am making a difference in the world.

The bottom line is: Talk to me. I am committed to creating win/wins in my life. Whatever your impression is of me, after reading this, you'll never know until you talk with me face to face. My commitment to you is that I am completely honest. Ask me anything.

● ● ●

Some cover letters are strangely brief:

I have 2+ years of database experience. If interested call me at (212)555-3597 in the evenings.

• • •

I am interested in receiving job offers in the following areas:

Security

Finance

Project Management

Sales and Distribution

Thank You

• • •

Please look at my resume and give me the answer.

• • •

Hello,

I am going to be on the market very soon.

Please find a position for me.

Thanks.

• • •

11
Disgruntled Creators

The resume of the "Disgruntled Creator" pays tribute to projects gone awry but not forgotten. Most "Disgruntled Creators" are burning a candle for projects that died prematurely - casualties of hard-line business objectives. Like Old Yeller, these projects had to be put down. We have more appreciation for "Disgruntled Creators" than just about any other job seekers in this book. "Disgruntled Creators" are about to snap, and we really can't blame them. Once upon a time, they served on projects that mattered; now they're stuck with the blandest work imaginable. Unfortunately, the resume is not the best vehicle to protest this state of affairs.

• • •

I was a nameless plebe, toiling mindlessly on projects that made no sense.

• • •

Concluding Remarks:

My main objective is to create a beautiful design for a project and make it work. This has been the cause of friction between me and upper management at several places, where they wanted to cut things short which would have destroyed the design.

• • •

Inferno Industries' strategy can be described simply as "hire 5 entry level programmers, and get a Star programmer for free," (me), and "by the time that poor sap wises up three years later hope you will have found another Star programmer for free." The company was started by four experienced programmers with no talent, that felt they had been screwed by their employers. A bad scene, one that I did not have the experience to avoid at all costs.

I worked on several programs that were eventually included in DOS-WINDOWS. I also worked on a great program that never saw the light of day.

• • •

• • •

I joined Strange Planet Entertainment as lead programmer in 1997. I was told that the way things worked is that you promise more than you can deliver to get the contract, hope you can actually deliver some of what you promised, and hope SPE does not get too upset when you are forced to scale back expectations halfway through the project.

• • •

92-95 ADVANCED DISTRIBUTED PROCESSOR TECHNOLOGY on MULTITASKING PLATFORM PROPOSAL, from the Brass Tacks to the System Engineering. Did analysis & prepared briefs on Customer Reponses to each presentation. (System shot down by Judge Redding, I damn near cried).

• • •

12
Let Me Be a Little More Specific

Precision can be very important in life. For example, if your grandmother was trying to tell you the location of some gold coins she buried in the backyard, you'd want to get some very detailed, specific information. Putting specifics on a resume, however, is a little trickier. How are we to know which ones will be of interest to hiring managers? Best bet: limit specifics to on-the-job details. The job seekers below opted for a different approach.

• • •

Sr. Director responsible for the North Florida Processing Division which oversees and provides systems and production support to the North Gulf Region profit centers. (North Gulf Region spans from Florida and Georgia state line heading west through Valdosta, GA to Tallahassee, FL and veers south to Ocala, FL then heads east through Orlando, FL all the way to Daytona, FL and straight back up north to the state line. Monticello, FL situates my regional head office).

• • •

Re Availability: East Coast and Canada: Phone on a Wednesday Night, confirm by e-mail immediately, and I'll be on the job at 7:00 AM the following Monday, no problem. (All can still be done later than listed below, but I will be beat when I get there!) I once got confirmation on a Friday at 2:30 PM and was on the job in Princeton, NJ a little before 7:00 AM the following Monday. Would have been easier (since I was pulling a U-Haul trailer), had I known not to use the Toll Road 300+ mile long parking lots! I know better now. It would also have been easier, had I not had to work over 14 hours minimum, seven days a week, including that Monday. But of course, I enjoyed it, strange?

• • •

Target opportunity: NET START UP. Interested in a Start-Up that knows what they want to achieve that needs someone to create the (Guru Level) Algorithm in Mathematical/Statistical/Logic Flow concepts that would enable a Coder to write the scripts. Also I would Mother/Guide/Promote the site operation. HOWEVER: If they Do-Not-Know what they need relative to Creative/Content/Techniques, specifically for "SELLING" Discounted Merchandise, as in THIS, I can beat anything/anyone out there, but we need to marry two different types of operations, which, again, I know who/what we need AND who/what is available. AND it hasn't been don't YET... Will consider OTHERS; relative to Creative/Content/Techniques, but this one I KNOW & NOW. But, of course, we need each-other, after all, we are interdependent! What more can I say, expect see my START-UP resume.

• • •

The $ topic: "Looking for the market salary for the job. Opportunity, challenge and potential is more important to me than initial salary. In the greater Cincinnati area I would deliberate on jobs less responsible beginning at $70,000; outside the Cincinnati area $85,000 adjusted by CPI, selective. As history and not to establish a requirement: of the half-dozen serious CIO and MIS Director interviews over the past year, have all been in the area of $108,000 at the Cost-of-Living index 100 level indexed for local living and tax cost level (Cincinnati is 95, San Francisco 165, New York 235, Little Rock 87 on the index). This amount agrees with the scale of the Federal government's Senior Executive Service. My job prior to organizing my own company, adjusted by cost-of-living increases, was $90,000 with bonus. I AM ONLY SEEKING A JOB AGREEING WITH MY EXPERIENCE; NOT INTERESTED IN BELOW TRACK RECORD JOBS; NO BIDDING WARS.

• • •

*This job seeker clearly overestimated the technical knowledge
(and the patience) of the average recruiter:*

Hi,

I have a small query if you guys could help me with. I use Access 97 as
my front-end to MS SQL-Server 6.5 which is my backend. I now plan to
upsize my entire MIS from Access 97 to Access 2000 same with SQL-
Server 6.5 to SQL-Server 7.0.

If I have to upsize I would like to know if Access 2000 supports a direct
query linkup to SQL 7.0 tables. E.g. : Can I just link SQL 7.0 tables to
Access 2000 like I did earlier using Access 97 with another Access.mdb
file? Will I have to write Parameterized Stored Procedures in Access
2000 or will the wizard do it for me?

I just read a newsletter from Microsoft on both the products, but can
you personally help me out?

I'm working as a Manager of MIS. Your feedback will be very important
in me making crucial decisions.

Waiting for help.

• • •

For the right job, I would be willing
to move from the Norwich area to
Northampton. Assuming I will be
living in Norwich or Northampton,
the place of work needs to be within
a 10 mile drive. I strongly prefer flex-
time, with the understanding that the
beginning of the day is by at least 10
am and the end of the day no earlier
than 4 pm. Natural light and good air
are extremely important to me. I'm
not extremely picky.

• • •

We like a bit of work-related detail on a resume, but this 18 page resume pushed that particular envelope. If your resume requires a table of contents to navigate, you've erred on the side of too much detail:

Table of Contents

• • •

Things I would like to see in a job:

Salary of at least 40K. The most I have made is 75K and the least I would consider is 30K, but for that low of a salary they would have to provide:

Awesome benefits.

Serious flexibility (like I get to work at home most of the time).

Really fun, interesting, challenging, and progressive work.

The greatest co-workers and office environment in existence.

• • •

This was a response on a registration form sent to a national placement agency:

Relocation Information: prefer bikeable distance from Amherst, MA.

• • •

13
Language Gaffes

Reading the same old grammatically-correct resume can be a real yawner. "Language Gaffes" freshen up the workmanlike prose of the resume. As it turns out, some resumes have humorous connotations and double meanings we do not intend. Most, but by no means all, of these funny language missteps are from folks who learned English as a second language. Now let's be clear: there's nothing funny about someone who takes on the challenge of mastering a new language and culture. That's why this category is a little less cautionary than the other sections in this book. If you're a foreign national, botching up your English a bit is not likely to cost you a job - unless you're applying to be a copy editor at *The New York Times*. So what you see below is not what we consider bad. It's more of an example of language nuances gone awry, with unintended humorous consequences.

> I am looking for a company that is driven to excellent.
>
> • • •

• • •

This email was in response to a career newsletter Rachel sent out:

Rachel,

I enjoyed the wonderful interview you mailed us this week and keep getting more and more enlightened by your tit bits!

Also let me know if position #SW02493 would work for me - I am very interested.

Thank you!

Mahendra

• • •

BS in Biology: Passed out in the year of 1995

Educational Qualification: Master Degree in Computer Applications (M.C.A) with First class (71%) from Numi Memorial College, Sumahara University, Bathri, passed out in the year of 1998. Bachelor Degree in Biology (B.Sc) with First class (69%) from Numi Memorial College, Sumahara University, Bathri, passed out in the year of 1995.

• • •

This was scrawled across the top of a cover letter written in French, from a job seeker applying for jobs in the U.S.:

Hi! I was very happy to receive news from your company and I join my Curriculum Vitae to this reply. I'm sorry that it is in French.

• • •

Dear Sir,

My past experience, and talks with friends gives me a feeling that I am perhaps the right man to get into ERP.

Please spare a few minutes to peep into my papers in the attachment and give me your feedback.

Hari

• • •

hello sir,

myself Manuel on line registered on 11-05-99

myself had attached my resume

you may kindly process it.

yourself and me will have constant touch with each other.

good day,

Manuel

• • •

A month later, I had pulled off enough impossible miracles that I was given cart-blank.

• • •

When I saw your ad in the paper, my eyeballs literally fell out!

• • •

Dear Mr. Jon Reed,

I'm a mechanical engineer with over 2 years of functional experience in Production Planning. I have also undergone training in Production Planning modules. I have gone through your pages in the net. I am really fascinated by you.

I need to get some real time experience, to come up in this field and I don't mind jumping jobs too, at least initially.

Is it possible for me.

Kindly clarify me.

Sincerely,

Jai Xua

• • •

This gentleman emailed his resume, received our company's auto-acknowledgement, and sent this baffling response. We hope his troubles are behind him:

Hi Rachel...

yes thank you for response... to help you... I qualify for engineering digital line (all kind) and telecomm wiring too... all kind...

All projects for cable (route) on poles lines etc.

Like: Lineman... foreman... contracts inspector...

I will tell you rachel Honestly... I'm starting to loose some (gaz)... also I thing gone loose my House... not a gift for my wife and kids...

I'm available from Canada to Japan... anywhere... and I will go alone... no problems with my wife... so I don't know...

Thank you to read me... HUM... Hum

Jacque Cretienne......

• • •

Extra Circular Activities

• • •

I'm a workhorse who doesn't wear horse-blinkers

Excellent communication skills are an added advantage.
Additional info: Availability and taking on challenging
projects most wud not take it up and play safe. A fast
learner who can pick up new concepts fast enuf to
implement for a project requirement. Highly dynamic and a
workhorse who DOESNT work wearing horse-blinkers!
THINKS SMART.

•••

Subject: A baseless Programmer with the simple secret knowledge in Programming, ready & energetic to become a striving part of a team with special goals.

• • •

I am a "people person", I don't like to alone.

• • •

To: Jobs

Subject: Composser Offer

Hi

My name is Francesco Rodriguez and I have experience in videogames industry like composser

if you are interested and want a demo music, dont doubt to contact to me.

regards

Francesco P. Rodriguez

• • •

To: Software Hiring Desk

RE: Crack Russian Software Programming Team Available Now!

• • •

A good moral builder

• • •

14
Informal Banter

No one would dream of wearing flip-flops to a job interview, but some of us achieve the electronic equivalent on our resumes by engaging in a kind of chit-chat we call "Informal Banter." Telling people we've never met that we "can get along with some partying," or that we "tend to get jumpy when things are slow," might fly in an AOL chat room, but it could ground a job search. Like it or not, the hiring process is still rife with formality. "Casual Fridays" might be an institution, but "Casual Resumes" aren't there yet.

• • •

93 VIDEO MAKER - Filmed/Produced 2 hr. movie, Raleigh, North Carolina, FX2X Corp. Then produced a successful sit-com which now resides in the Jimmy Carter Center Library. My friend Randy T. got fired 30 days before Sit-Com Production Contract.

• • •

Challenge. I really like a good challenge. The problem with that is that when I haven't experienced any particular challenge, I don't always know exactly how long it will take to complete, so how do I come up with a deadline? Boring work brings out restlessness in me and when I find myself bored at work, I often take on a side job that challenges me and creates progressive learning. Cutting edge work and risk are for me.

• • •

I am way more of a hut in the wilderness than a jet set in NY City (would you believe that???) but I can still get along with some partying, that is IF I get my silence in the morning.

• • •

My priorities are family then work and have been described as a work-aholic by my peers. I enjoy coaching soccer and playing chess for hobbies and don't drink or smoke but it does not bother me when others do.

• • •

Personality and other stuff:

If your are still reading this, my guess is you probably do have something in mind for me... so stick a bit longer... you might just learn something interesting...

I like when things are moving (fast and forward hopefully), and I tend to get jumpy when things are slow (inaction melts my brain cells).

• • •

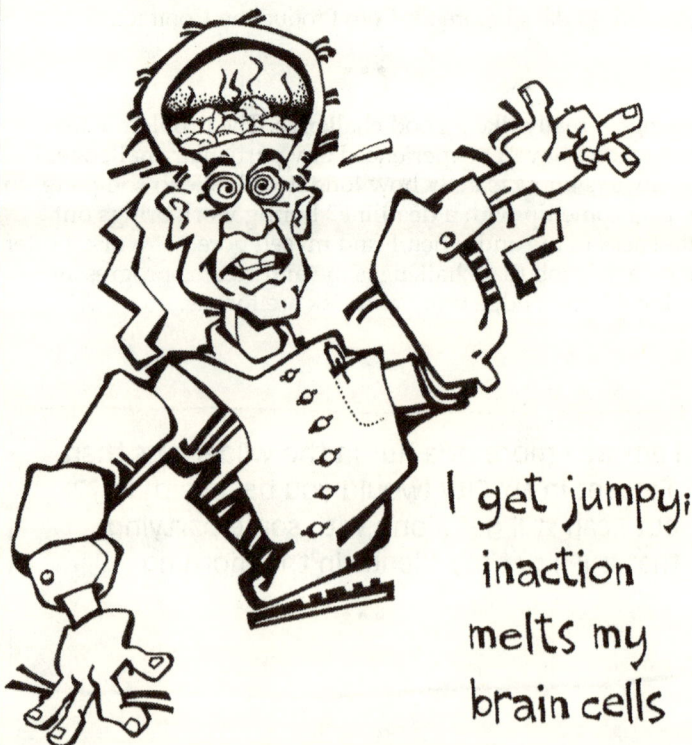

I get jumpy; inaction melts my brain cells

My completed work, The Executive Station, enables the user to

* Set global product sales quotas.

* Produce multiple sells (I will spare you the details), attendance, cost effectiveness, and inventory reports.

* Program sales variation based on dates, day of weeks, and product category.

* And a lot more that I unfortunately can not remember just now.

• • •

May 1998 to November 2000

Handy Head-Hunters

Programmer

Customers and resources table with match engine on criteria based on skills. Generates resume in Doc, TXT, XL, HTML format. Web enabled. Who knows, I might just start one of those businesses myself.

• • •

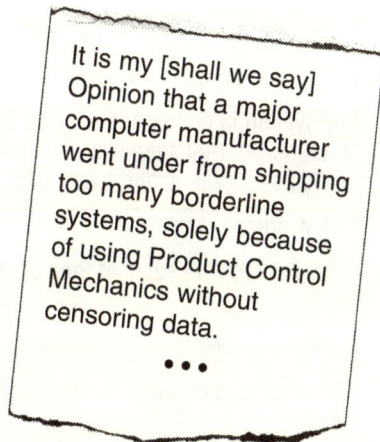

It is my [shall we say] Opinion that a major computer manufacturer went under from shipping too many borderline systems, solely because of using Product Control Mechanics without censoring data.

• • •

Xanadu Project

1994 - ?

Eugene, OR

Programmer - Analyst

Description:

This dude seems to be a life-quest for me... at 24-years-old that's the closest thing I have to a baby... It's basically a web based game to conquer the universe. I can't say more just yet.

• • •

Here is a series of statements for you to overview. They are brief and direct and only designed to save you a little time. There is always a chance to succeed further together! I can not do a project by myself, but I am smart enough to know a large project can not be completed without an experienced-friendly-open-interactive team. Kind of like me! --! Experienced, open, friendly and interactive!!??? PLUS I like the X-Files!

• • •

The following are projects that I am currently working on.

You might want to skip to next page (the numbered projects section) to get the ones that are done and over with (if that really exists).

Sales and Inventory Management System

C, C++, Visual C++ Programmer

The system is composed of sales terminals (at the actual McBurgers restaurants), management PC (where the actual software sits), products, suppliers and transactions.

This program is used to:

* Set pricing for seasonal food promotions (most of the tricky stuff is here).

* Program special meal discounts (the rest of the tricky stuff is here).

* Monitor and override burger availability status in real-time (piece off cake).

* Produce a huge array of reports (McBurgers is actually summing up every g of mayonnaise that sits in your burger, I swear). Unfortunately, it is not within my rights to give you guys any more details.

• • •

It would make sense that if you are going to spend the majority of your life working to fulfill your desires, you should have a job that both fulfills your desires while making money to put back into those desires you so wish to fulfill. *smiles*

• • •

Then all of a sudden the Internet comes along and overnight local families, businesses, and educational folks seem to know "all about everything." Funny how that is, huh? One true fact is: most anyone who owns a computer loves to play games or enjoys some form of recreation so that is why your ad "STIMULATED MY ELECTRONIC VISUAL NEURONS!" I believe your company has an exceptional mission, now all we have to figure out is how to get the job done!

• • •

Integrated Sales Terminals and Inventory System

Programmer / Analyst

This is actually a remake of a previous project. I could not resist the urge to do it again but with a nice GUI this time (Foxpro is really brutal).

• • •

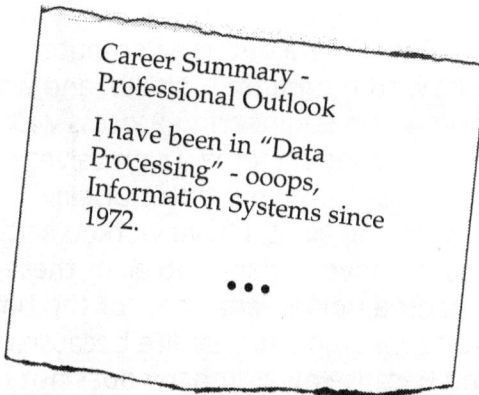

Career Summary -
Professional Outlook

I have been in "Data Processing" - ooops, Information Systems since 1972.

• • •

Most of the time I am in disguise...
4 years have passed this way

Briefly speaking, I came out as a Computer Professional with Programming skills, and walked through the whole Engineering Process with the inferiority of a failed Diploma. From valves through RCN, to the latest trend in Graphic Display Interfaces with the Plant, I have worked a little bit in everything. I have understood all of these, but am not a Degree Holder, and most of the time I am in disguise suppressing all that life because of a failure, and because my Company does not develop software... 'Four' years have passed this way.

• • •

15
Sounding Off: Voice Mails from Hell

Now it's time to meet some folks who put a voice to the blunders we've laid out. As you're about to see, these job seekers take categories like "Language Gaffes," "Informal Banter," and "Too Much Information" to a whole new level. Our voice mail system gave callers up to five minutes to say their piece - enough time for some pretty creative performances. Here are the transcripts of a few we saved.

• • •

"Hey Listen, guys, I was trying to call DP Dough, but I got you guys, and I'm really baked, so I was just calling to say your number is so much like DP Dough's! But I do need a job, man, because I'm going out to California and stuff. But give me a call back, the number is 555-8659. Nice talking to you guys. You guys should really change that number though because I was really trying to get DP Dough. See you later!"

• • •

"Hi Rachel, how are you? This is Crevier... We have spoken before... we spoke on a day when you were dropping somebody off at the airport and it snowed cats and dogs... does that refresh your memory? I believe not. Give me a call tomorrow when you get a chance at 215-555-4599. Thank you, Rachel."

• • •

"Hey Rachel, hey this is Brian. Um, yeah, I called the hiring manager at Softrix back, and told her that if she wants to try to reach me after 1:00 her time that I'd be here until 5:00... so maybe she will, maybe she won't. So I said, well, if she wants to interview me Thursday, um, like, after 10:30, I think she said, I said that would be fine too. So, I'm just hanging out, and waiting for a call. So in the mean time, I hope you're having a good day. I'm stuffed. I just, like, pigged out. Huge lunch. There's this place that makes great subs, that are just, like, huge. But anyway. So that's sort of the update. Bye."

• • •

Jon, I'll call you back later...

This consultant called in from the road on his cell phone, which was shorting out intermittently. Fortunately, it was his wife, not him, at the wheel:

... [various highway sounds and a crackling cell phone connection...] "Hey Jon... I got your email and that job is right up my alley! The only issue [-----------------------] I could be a problem because I know that manager from Hitachi and he [----------------------------]... Right now we're driving back from Phoenix and I should be back in Santa Fe by 8 o'clock and [------------------]... Look out!!!" [HONKING SOUNDS, SCREECH OF TIRES]... "Oh shit!!!!! [--------------------] Right of way!! [--------------------] ... Jon... OK. OK? OK... Yes, I'll call him back. Jon, I'll call you back later."

• • •

"Hello Jon Reed. I am pleased to make your electronic acquaintance. We have not spoken before, but I am the dead-on perfect fit for your project management position on the west coast you featured on your web site. I am not sure what city that is in; I am based out of Sacramento but I can travel to anywhere from L.A. to San Francisco. You will undoubtedly be pleased to know that I have already implemented PeopleSoft in a high tech setting before, and I've configured the specific sales order functionality for that industry your client is looking for. I will be available as of the 1st of April and my presence can be requested for an interview on any Friday with a week's notice, and an ample briefing from you on the company in advance of my appointment. I hope this verbal overview tickled your interest in a mutual arrangement. I look forward to talking with you at your first convenience."

(This caller got so wrapped up in his verbal presentation that he forgot to leave his name or phone number. Jon never heard from him again.)

• • •

"Jonny Boy!

I just sent you my revised resume tonight. Your suggestions were ALL right on. That's tough love, my man, but I'm glad you gave me a push. It felt really good to get this done… like taking a REALLY good crap. Maybe that was a bad analogy… [soft chuckling]. OK, call me. It's Larry."

• • •

"Jon - Mark. I got your message an hour ago. I just got back from the interview… it went a bit longer than I thought. I stayed and talked to Michael about whether he'd get pulled into the south region with me. Jon, it went well. But Jon, I have to tell you, I liked what they had to say, but I need them to really blow my skirt up. They haven't blown my skirt up yet. I want to talk to you and find out what you think they'll give me. They want me, but are they playing with the big boys? It takes more than a kiss on the cheek to get me to the prom, Jon. Call me tonight. Bye."

• • •

"Jon, Steve Gilroy here... Got the offer by fax an hour ago... I'm still choking on the fumes... don't they know what the going rate is for EDI? Jon, I'm getting an offer tomorrow that's going to blow this one out of the water... that's bad news for your commission. This offer has fine print galore... if I take a Snickers from the mini-bar it comes off my billables... looks like you've got a second-tier client on your hands. See if you can get me an extra 10K per quarter and a billable hours bonus anytime I go over forty and then we can talk. Tell 'em I don't come cheap and every dollar to me is ten off their bottom line. I'm out."

• • •

"Jon, this is Dr. Patrick Nightingale. I received your inquiry earlier today, along with some preliminary details on a Lotus Notes position in New Jersey that you are evidently considering me for. Jon, if you are familiar with the history of Lotus Notes, then you are already familiar with my credentials. I was part of the original Lotus Notes development team; I was instrumental in designing a product that is considered vastly superior to all other groupware solutions. When IBM acquired Lotus Notes, IBM executives were panicked that I would leave the team, leaving them without the brainpower behind the acquisition - which I did. As an independent Lotus Notes consultant, I can offer abilities to clients that you cannot find, not to mention intellectual capital that only those of us who developed the solution could have. Compensation is simple to resolve, once you are familiar with my requirements. You may set up the billing arrangements to your convenience, but understand that I will be expecting $100 an hour on a W-2 hourly basis, and by that, I mean $100 an hour 'net to me.' You calculate the deductions to reach my magic number; I go to your client and perform miracles. Please call me to finalize these arrangements and set up a meeting with your client. As you know, I can be reached at 978-555-7677."

• • •

16
The Odd Self-Sell

The folks in this section have the right idea about self-marketing, but they pushed the resume a little farther than it can go. They could learn a thing or two from Bruce Willis. When Bruce auditions for new movie roles, he doesn't say, "Oh, by the way, I did a great album of blues standards in '87, and I'd love to contribute something to the soundtrack." He has the good sense to save the promotion of *The Return of Bruno* for another time. We should all take similar precautions when composing our resumes and cover letters.

• • •

I am intent on moving into Oracle consulting and have taken the Apps and DBA training. I have been able to bootleg time on a system here in Houston to gain experience and know enough to be dangerous now, however the people at the site are keeping me from running rampant before I cause a meltdown. They will graciously give me a good recommendation, if for no other reason than to keep me from pestering them with questions.

• • •

My biggest weaknesses are looking at things with an overly optimistic view, overloading myself with commitments, and restlessness with non-challenging projects. This causes problems when I am estimating time and resources for a project, working on an open-ended project, or doing grunt-work.

• • •

> **Education: Completed all coursework for MS, alas, no degree.**
>
> • • •

For seven years, I led 1/8 of all program activities for 1900 local Mensans, including their IBM-PC special interest group.

• • •

Created assembly language virus that spreads through .NET files without affecting their execution, resides in unused area of the secondary vector table, scrambles all DNS entries, and unscrambles them on the fly. Never released in wild.

• • •

Single, 43, mid-career change service industry executive. No formal schooling in graphic design. Dad died, re-located to Vermont to maintain family property. Adobe Illustrator certified corporate instructor.

• • •

(Note: Ranked by U.S. Bureau of Measurement & Standards in upper 1/20 of 1% nationally for cognitive reasoning.) Self-taught since high school.

• • •

French is my natural language but I speak and write English fluently. I do know a little Japanese and some Spanish, but not enough to be worth while.

• • •

Integrated Sales and Inventory System

Programmer - Analyst

Description:

All life cycles of analysis, debugging, and deployment phases. I was alone.

I have completed 3
hours towards my MBA.

• • •

To achieve maximum qualifications for your firm, I agree to work FOR FREE for one year as a "remote" employee of your firm and connect with you by means of email. Also, I will master the field in which you direct me.

• • •

Summary
WARNING: I am a very out going individual. Confident with myself and my abilities, I will succeed at all tasks required of me. Along with my experience, I bring innovation and dedication. Due to my energetic nature, I seek out challenges and enjoy the struggle of new tasks.

• • •

I created and invented the use of the "legal opinion letter" and "promotional conduct handbook" used in advertising today. The promotional handbook forces the Federal Communications Commission (FCC) to file only Commercial Fraud indictments against advertisers like myself instead of Capital Fraud which carries jail time.

• • •

Current situation: I am a senior manager in a productive environment, but, sadly, I can't say the same of my colleagues. Because the other biz units did not hit their numbers, I did not get part of my plan (bonus)! Not only that, but I now get to work another 3 years to realize any hope of options. When mediocrity is rewarded and excellence disregarded, it's time to make a move.

• • •

Included in my resume materials is my picture from the Pirate's Cove game for which I did my cross platform work. Compare this to my lack of a picture in the Medieval Times credits, not to mention removing my real job title and placing my credit below even coffee girl, and that should make it obvious that I was screwed over by these people. Which should also point out that I am a first class lead programmer others fear.

• • •

Things that are important to me: Ingenuity, brilliance, and people who are the best at what they do. Completely honest and timely communication. And people who like to have fun while they get things done.

Other things I like are: Flexibility, both personality wise and time wise. When I get on a roll I can easily work all night. My experience is that flexibility works really well when communication is honest and open. I like to stay ahead of schedule so that when events (trainings, lectures, reunions, social events, etc.) are presented, it's OK to be there and experience them and know that it doesn't detract from work.

• • •

This gentleman submitted a resume for a female friend of his:

Please see if you can explore the possibilities of getting her a job. She has done her Lawson Financials. She is good technically in Powerbuilder and RISC 2000. She is also very good in Word and PowerPoint. She is also a professional dancer!

• • •

Have written short stories for a year as a passion. Have been published in Bradbury's Sci-Fi magazine. Also I have a bad habit of being loyal beyond stupidity and am dedicated to the relentless pursuit of perfection.

• • •

Personal Home Page on Compuserve is a good example of my work (having been created without the benefit a Graphic Interface to the NET!) Given the proper tools, it would have Audio attributes, as well as Motion Video capabilities.

• • •

16
Makin' Friends with Recruiters

Is it worth the trouble to "make nice" with the recruiters in your life? The folks in this "Makin' Friends" chapter don't seem to think so - although some of their miscues are likely due to a lack of understanding of the recruiter's role. If the recruiters you work with have strong ties to hiring managers (and the best recruiters have exclusive access to certain jobs), making nice might not be such a bad idea, even if the headhunters you deal with make you want to take a shower when you hang up the phone.

For better or worse, recruiters serve as the initial screener and interviewer for the job openings our clients have asked us to fill. Ultimately, we decide which applicants to present to our clients. Once we've determined that an applicant has achieved the "skills threshold," interpersonal skills emerge as a key criteria. So the more we like you (and your skills), the harder we'll work on your behalf - typically at no cost to you, the job seeker. On the other hand, if we don't think so much of your charms, we might keep your resume to ourselves.

When you're dealing with recruiters, it's also helpful to keep in mind that most of us are paid on a commission-only basis - no placements, no food on the table. The implications? We don't have gobs of time to chat with folks whose skills lie outside our area of specialization, and we don't make the best (or the most cooperative) market research assistants. The recruiting process comes down to a draw: the recruiter needs the cooperation of the job seeker, and the job seeker needs the cooperation of the recruiter. That's why we scratch our heads when a job seeker opts to kick off the relationship by sending us a list of things for us to "Google" for them, or by aggressively questioning our practice of using a database to manage our contacts. And for the record, BOSSING US AROUND IN ALL CAPS, or informing us that we face stiff competition from all the other recruiters who are scrapping for the same commission, are not the best motivational tactics.

• • •

This person wrote in after receiving an automated email response thanking him for his resume and letting him know we'd be in touch when we found a relevant opportunity:

Rachel:

I am somewhat confused when you respond to me that you will review my background... my background I already know is quite good. I am not looking for someone to "add me to their database" for a possible match in the future.

Could you have someone contact me from your firm so that we can discuss my future in more detail (and not have me sit electronically in your system)??? I know that your firm would profit greatly if you placed me, so I am a little upset when I read things like this!!!

Thanks,

Christopher

• • •

Some job seekers think of recruiters as volunteer research assistants. The following three emails are indicative of this approach:

Dear Mr. John Reed!!

Could you please explain the following terms!!

* Logo Partners * Implementation Partners * Platform Partners * Database partners * development partners * Integration partners * complimentary partners * software and other partners

Please do the needful!!

• • •

Dear Mr. Reed,

I would like to build my knowledge in the following areas. Kindly provide me with the relevant information regarding the following points:

1. ERP as a concept

2. Applicability of ERP in industries

3. Major Players of ERP

4. ERP as a Career path.

Also provide me with the best Internet Site addresses for footnoting each point of information.

• • •

Jon:

I would like to know more details about Informix opportunities. Will you please e-mail me the info like the rates depending on the location and experience. I would like to see the info in the form of a table showing years of experience, geographical region and rate.

Thanks.

• • •

Re: Salary requirement reduction.

Recruiter:

My minimum salary is $14.00 hourly, but try for more!

Try hard to sell them on the idea of hiring me. I am highly experienced, and will be a great benefit to their company with my abilities. I need to work NOW.

Avoid industrial electronic assignments dealing with high voltage, 4-phase power, motors, servo systems, or large machines.

• • •

This individual sent a mass email to all the recruiters he was working with. Since a recruiter's chances of placing someone go down with each additional recruiter the job seeker is working with, his approach was curious, to say the least:

This message is going out to everyone that I've contacted over the last 30 to 45 days by means of Headhunter.net

Anyone who is presently in a negotiation with me, and you know who you are, everything is on track, and hopefully we'll eventually see eye-to-eye.

OTHERWISE...

If I sent you the URL for my resume, and you never took the time to look it over, then I'm seriously scratching my head. Between Thanksgiving, when I put my resume online, and today, when I'm "tickling" (reminding) all of you that I exist, the US Geek Gap has grown by another 68,000 open, unfilled jobs, to 432,000.

• • •

Some job seekers ask recruiters for help handling job offers that the recruiter has no stake in or knowledge of:

Comments: I have offers from E&Y and Anderson Consulting and an interview scheduled at KPMG. I have to let them know my decision today (time now is 4:00 a.m. in the morning) and I need help making the decision. I am a very hard-working, self-motivated, enthusiastic person. I would like to talk to you or another concerned person. If you can give me a call before noon I would greatly appreciate it. E&Y has been waiting for my answer for 3 weeks and Anderson for 2 weeks. I have to let both of them know my decision 100% today. My phone is (717)555-5634. I will be looking forward to talk to you.

• • •

Another example of a job seeker asking us for advice on a job placement that's already been made. Perhaps recruiters would respond to this type of approach better if they didn't work on straight commission:

Sirs,

I have been given a placement with a company who call themselves as LIA (Logistics Information Applications) from the U.S. holding an office in the address stated below.

I kindly request you to furnish me the details of the following aspects pertaining to the company & their status as of now in the U.S. to enable me to make a decision of signing the agreement letter.

1. Confirmation & Checking on the genuineness of the company.

2. How long have they been operating this business & are they well known, popular and trustworthy.

3. How big is their organization/company in the U.S. (i.e. number of people working and consultants).

4. The LIA has asked me to pay Rs. 10 Lakhs to undergo training with them in India.

I request you to e-mail as early as possible as the deadline for signing the agreement papers is given to me as 22.3.99

• • •

*This job seeker assumed that we would be eager to help him
go directly to the clients we represent and cut ourselves out of
the loop:*

Thank you for the reply. I would like to get in touch
with The Big Six firms in New York, USA. Could you
send me their EMAIL ADDRESSES IMMEDIATELY?

• • •

17
Silly Skills

Does having access to a "fax mailbox" give you an edge over other applicants? And what the heck is "Verbal Karate"? These are just a couple of the questions raised when people broaden their resumes to include the most tangential (or self-evident) human accomplishments. Before we proceed, we need to acknowledge that the "Silly Skills" category can get a little touchy, as some of the humor is clearly related to the differences in assumed knowledge between white collar and blue collar workers. Here's how we look at it: a resume can only be bad (and funny bad) if it impedes your job search and puts off hiring managers. Therefore, the kind of position being targeted has a lot to do with the humor. For example, a food service worker who has computer literacy could be a real asset in an increasingly wired workplace. Nothing funny about a resume like that. But a white-collar worker selling us on their abilities to load up a fax machine and hit the send button might be pushing it. Your authors both have arduous and proud food service backgrounds, so please don't call the humor police when we point out that if you're applying for white collar/managerial positions - as was the case for all of the applicants featured below - then perhaps it's time to drop the details of assembling sandwiches and dishwasher tray operation off the resume.

● ● ●

I am an expert in Verbal Karate with experience teaching F.B.I. agents and tough homicide detectives how to interrogate suspects!

● ● ●

> **Hardware: Laser Printer, Fax Machine, Mouse, Keyboard, Monitor, Mainframe, Microcomputer**
>
> ● ● ●

Telepresence

Voice messaging, fax mailbox, direct phone to my desk.

• • •

I'm not a geek, except when I want people to think I am. I can talk about things other than computers, and I wear a suit well.

• • •

This person was applying for positions in the U.S. with no foreign-language requirements:

I prefaced my letter to you with one in German so that a German-speaking member at your office can see that I do speak (and write) in fluent German.

• • •

This gentleman listed all of his college classes on his resume, including:

Golf and Bowling I

• • •

Arranging chairs and tables for various school occasions, washing dishes, putting dishes and silverware into the dishwasher cycle, removing leftovers from trays, changing trash, wiping the tray belt line.

• • •

Cooking meat, assembling sandwiches, steaming bread, changing trash, sweeping floors, wiping tables, mopping floors, putting perishables in proper racks.

• • •

Intangibles: Finely-Calibrated BS meter

18
If You Don't Ask, I Will:
The Self-Questionnaire

Resumes and cover letters are just not interactive enough for some folks. But there's an ingenious/problematic solution: the self-questionnaire. If the goal is to stand out from one's peers, then the self-questionnaire is a pole vault into the view of the hiring manager. We've seen some interesting self-questionnaires over the years, including the technical self-exam which the applicant submitted voluntarily, but failed to pass. Is it possible to question yourself on a resume without heading into deep waters? Judging from the following, that's one question that remains unanswered.

• • •

Confidential Resume:

A Methodology to dominate 45% of Ebusiness Market

How?

My strategic methodology requires a lot of IT resources. The small company might not handle it enough. If your senior executive board thinks that your company handles it, you can contact me.

Why don't I just focus my own business with my own methodology?

To be honest with you,

1st Reason: God gave me the great idea as a gift, and I do not want to lose the great idea itself.

2nd Reason: My status is very limited since… (I can tell you via email). I am now ready to be selling myself with the methodology, which can easily conquer one third of the Ebusiness market.

How much do I believe that it would be successful?

1200%. However, you must give me a time, at least for next three years. I need 3 years to dominate some piece of the e-business pie. If it is unsuccessful, I will return all of my salary until my employment expires.

• • •

Keep in mind that the following self-questionnaire, like the rest in this section, was designed and submitted by the applicant:

Previous Employment:

1. Please list your recent compensation history, and exact dates of employment, if not included on your resume.

Please see resume.

2. Is there anything missing or incorrect about your resume?

Please see resume.

• • •

Perhaps this applicant should have customized his questionnaire to fit his professional experience:

Training Matrix:

Please indicate formal training classes given by Oracle that you have attended and date attended.

Class Name	Date Attended	Location

Please indicate certification levels within Oracle that you have achieved and the accompanying date.

Module Name	Date Achieved	Certification Level

Q: Which Oracle Suite(s) are you most comfortable delivering consulting services in?

A: None of the new Suites.

_____

_____

_____

_____

Q: Have you had any implementation experience with Oracle Manufacturing?

A: Unfortunately, no.

_____

_____

_____

_____

Q: Please indicate your familiarity with the Oracle "Quick Start" Methodology.

A: None.

_____

_____

_____

_____

Q: Please indicate your familiarity with the Oracle DBA Methodology.

A: None.

_____

_____

_____

_____

• • •

When do you want to start a new position?

Within the next couple months. There is a special consideration I should point out, and that is an extended trip I am planning the end of June through the first week in July. It is a personal goal I have set for myself, and while personal goals might not seem to be an important factor in regards to the workplace, my experience as a military CO has shown me that a troop who has personal satisfaction is a better worker. With that in mind, I would like a position that I could start before that time and come back to, or perhaps start afterwards.

(The reaction of the hiring manager to someone who volunteers this kind of vague information? Set it aside and see if they re-apply with a bit more focus after their "extended" trip.)

• • •

This gentleman is the victim of his own redundancy:

B. Do you require relocation assistance, or would you relocate on your own for the right job? Explain.

I have relocated myself within a thousand miles before. I do not have a great deal of personal property as I live in an apartment, but I do have a car and full-size motorcycle to transport.

C. Do you have a house to sell before you relocate, or do you rent?

Refer to previous answer.

• • •

19
Warriors and Alpha Dogs

Businesses love metaphors... ("Jim, that sales pitch was a slam dunk!" "Lisa, you hit one out of the park with that PowerPoint demo!") On some level, these analogies make sense - what is business if not glorified competition? But when we start comparing business to war itself, that might be pushing it. The folks below are willing to push it. Meet the "Warriors and Alpha Dogs." Their resumes put us on notice: once hired, they'll take over the team from their "less gifted teammates," and go about securing their place in the corner office. In theory, self-confidence can be an asset in our job search. But effective resumes thrive on a certain kind of modesty. When our resume starts barking, we might be turning into "Alpha Dogs."

• • •

This job seeker was applying for a computer gaming position:

Give me a video game you think you're good at and I'll give you a bruised ego. Give me any video game and in ten minutes I'll beat you at it. Give me any fighting game and I'll beat you without an ounce of practice.

• • •

The company that I choose to associate with (other than my own), better well be an extraordinary visionary entrepreneurial operation. I'll treat a vested position as my own: with great pride coupled with unwavering dedication to its prosperity. I have an exceptional sense of humor to share with those around me!

• • •

I am 6 foot 6 inches tall, and have a commanding presence.

I am an exceptionally high achiever and a workaholic. I am thirty-six years old, in excellent health, happily married with children, am six-foot-six inches tall, and have a commanding presence. I earned my doctorate at the age of twenty-two.

• • •

Suffolk Group/Integrated Technologies

Sr. Production Engineer (1981 - 1985)

Suffolk hired me through a mentor/customer at ALC. They flew me out and gave me the tour with the Operations Manager. The President then took me aside and said, "What do we need?" I recommended what is now called Enterprise Computing.

• • •

WHO: Dynamic Sales & Marketing WARRIOR LEADER - MBA - over 15 years experience

WHY ME: If you view Sales & Marketing like a WAR then you need a WARRIOR

WHAT CAN I DO: "Take Charge Change Agent and WARRIOR LEADER"

• • •

As I hold others to my high standards, I sometimes have to step up and lead the effort or just give someone the tools to enjoy the success of the team. I can make a difference between profit and loss. I am the WIN-WIN manager.

11/1998 - Present

Company: Confidential

Job title: Future Dominator of E-Business World

• • •

• • •

My uncanny ability to predict early in a project what will, and especially what will not, satisfy user requirements has already saved my Federal and commercial clients hundreds of millions of dollars. I have also excelled at delivering solutions to "impossible" problems after repeated failures by others.

• • •

I have provided enthusiastic leadership to software development and rollout teams. Once, I inherited a "dirty dozen" team of misfits, each of whom were to be fired at the project's conclusion. Six months later, my team had improved their job performance and team attitude so dramatically that they were retained at the project's conclusion while the five other teams lost half of their members instead.

• • •

To Whom It May Concern:

I seek a vested executive marketing / sales or management position with an agile firm on the verge of an IPO or major expansion. I'm a highly motivated statesman with a disarming commanding presence. I'm a very strong closer and prefer to sell to CEOs and top decision makers. I take great pride in my ability to develop strong sincere rapport with individuals before and after the sale. This innate visionary ability sets me apart from most people. I cultivate deep lasting relations that transcend

I would like to introduce myself. I am age 22 years and 5'9". I am a handsome, dynamic, ambitious, outspoken person with great communication skills.

• • •

Experience: Consultant and body shop work
since 1972. Have led development teams for
proprietary manufacturing systems and
Windows/DOS applications. Consistently
successful. I succeed where others fail.

• • •

transactions. I relish public speaking, training people and the
art of negotiation.

• • •

In the management arena, I have originated and developed
marketing leads. I have written winning proposals for federal and
commercial contracts - I later negotiated and balanced their
budgets and schedules. I am an extrovert, and because of my
exceptional ability to express myself, I have even delivered client
presentations for projects other than my own to help my less
gifted teammates.

• • •

Once, after a company's six man team exhausted their
$400,000 budget over sixteen months without
producing any results, the furious contracting officer
threatened to have the company placed on the
government's "debarred" list, essentially putting the
entire company out of business for four years. I then
personally took over the entire project, and in just
two months delivered the 125 Assembler modules and
the Biological Warfare Model to the surprised and
grateful customer.

• • •

74-89 QA/JPC ENGINEERING GROUP: Authored Group(s) Dept. Quality
Assurance Director: Originate or Review All Sys., Eng. Procedures&

Policies. CA. Initiated a coordination method which got all groups working together. Lived in plant (slept in cot) during major audits...

• • •

This person's resume listed his employer's competitors for each work experience:

1987-1991

Retail Consulting, Inc.

Regional Account Manager

Customer Base: Wal-Mart, Victoria's Secret, Filene's, Lord & Taylor

Competition: IBM, PriceWaterhouse

1991 - Present

Documentation Systems Inc.

National Account Manager

Customer Base: AT&T, Arthur Anderson, Proctor & Gamble, Dean Whitter, Fortune Accounts

Competition: The World

• • •

20
Sloganeers

It's kind of neat to coin a phrase that promotes our image…
"Hammer Time!" That's why some job seekers look at the
white space at the top of their resumes and salivate. But in
reality, "Sloganeers" might be better off renting out that
space to Office Max or Pizza Hut. "Sloganizing a resume" sets
up a conflict between the ego of the individual and the ego of
the employer. Once we're on the job, we'll be expected to tone
down our personal branding initiative, and embrace the
corporate mission and slogans. No, slapping on a slogan isn't
the worst thing you can do to a resume. But we're going to
wait until someone successfully pulls it off before we start
creating slogans for our own resumes.

• • •

Breckenridge James (Breck) Sherman

Specializing in the Impossible

• • •

Jeff P. Fielding

A Team Player Who Will Put Your Company In The Best Light
And Never Do Anything You Will Have to
Apologize For Or Have To Defend

• • •

Frank B. Samuelson

Developer, Designer and Pusher of the Envelope

• • •

Daniel Brown

Have Passport & Don't Use Tobacco or Firearms

• • •

Nate Jackson

Inventing Better Ideas for Better Results for Better Living for Better Happiness

• • •

Personal: Enjoy Dim Sum, Chai and other good things in life: "Tell me what you DON'T eat, and I'll tell you who you are."

• • •

21
Politics, Religion, and Other Inappropriate Subjects

If your goal is simply to call attention to yourself, there's no better tactic than the opinion-laden resume. But here's the quandary: no client has ever said to us, "Find us someone who can really serve up politics and religion at the water cooler." Even the best companies have red tape somewhere - they're not scouring their inboxes for the next Erin Brokovich. Don't get us wrong, we like people with conviction. But we also like people who understand that not everyone has the exact same viewpoints as they do.

• • •

I founded LineShare in 1992 after IBM turned down the business plan and moved to Tucson, Arizona. LineShare was the Premier 1-900- dial-around provider in Nevada. I did everything at LineShare at some time: network design, switch maintenance, customer service, you name it. Regulatory reform (sic?) in 1996 at both the State and Federal level has forced me out of the teleprovider role, but I can recycle the entrepreneurial experience as we move forward into the Information Age.

• • •

Though the right opportunity might not be available for several months, I'm willing to wait for the right situation. I'm 42, have a wonderful wife and two sons, and love Jesus Christ with all my heart.

• • •

Dear Sir/Madam:

I wish to work for a company that respects the taxpayer (if government contracting). I truly believe that what happened on election day, November 8, 1994, was neither an accident nor a joke, and I hope to contribute to necessary missions and fat-cutting efforts that will hopefully be the new trend. I tell you up front that I am a conservative who tries to live up to traditional values, firmly believing that is the best way to serve my fellow man (as well as my employer and my customer).

• • •

Dear sirs,

Thanks a lot for your reply.

May I learn from you the names of companies that would hire me directly?

Will you be kind and give me an opportunity at such a company which is known to you?

May I wish Human love (Real GOD) in between us?

Yes! Existence of love and truth will be forever due to persons like you in the Universe.

Venkat,

Lovely Human being.

• • •

Dress codes seem superfluous and dishonest

Flexibility. The more they pay me, the more benefits and flexibility I am willing to let go. But even with all of that, I really like flexibility of time. An important part of my life is trainings and seminars. I like to take a day or two when these kind of things come up, and not have to worry that somebody might not like it. I like "crunch time" when there are a few days of really intense completion work, and then I like to take some time to be with my family. The politics of large companies is OK when necessary, but not my ideal choice. I like to sometimes work a "swing" or "mid" shift on my own for a while. Dress codes seem superfluous and dishonest. Rather than force an outside appearance, inspire personal adherence to a personal dress code, and inspire higher standards.

• • •

Whether or not the United States government chooses to play a leadership role in the expansion of free trade within the western hemisphere and throughout the world, participation in international commerce will be vital to the continued existence and success of corporate entities. This intrigues me, and I have worked hard to prepare myself for a career in international business.

• • •

22
Hostile Email Interactions

As you might suspect, not all job seekers take rejection lightly. On the contrary: some of them take the news of a bad skills match very personally. No matter how nicely you phrase it, sometimes when you tell someone they're not qualified for a job, feathers get ruffled. If you've been waiting to see the authors get a taste of our own medicine, look no further than these "make my day" emails we received over the years. They say you shouldn't dish it out if you can't take it. Well, as these letters prove, we've taken our fair share of it. If you want to generate this kind of hostility in your email inbox, it's not hard: simply send someone an email thanking them for their resume, tell them they're not qualified, and wish them good luck. If you make the email extra nice, you just might get an extra special response back.

• • •

These two applicants didn't appreciate the news that the jobs they applied for required work experience in the United States:

Hi Jon,

Thanks for your mail... which looked/read more like a circular drafted for mass distribution!

I fail to understand as to what is so special about J.D. Edwards projects in the U.S. In fact, what you mean to say by this is that people who have worked on J.D. Edwards projects outside the U.S. do not know anything!

I would like this opportunity to tell you that J.D. Edwards is being implemented throughout the globe.

In fact, you should have posted this information on your web page so that people do not unnecessarily send their resumes to you guys.

I hope you found this email informative.

• • •

Dear Jon,

I do appreciate the trouble you went into, by explaining why you cannot find a job for somebody that is... well, I am really not sure in what category of "sorry I cannot help you" I fall into, since I do have solid experience.

The advertisements on your web site say you basically employ anybody, even people that don't have any hands-on experience. So I am really at a loss understanding what exactly you are trying to explain.

It just so happens that I came back from an implementation in Chicago, so I do know what you mean when you say "American Standards," believe me, they are non-existing in comparison with the standards I am used to here in Germany.

I would like to remind you as well that Germany has been implementing ERP systems over the last ten years, before the mighty USA woke up to it in 1993.

I sincerely hope that your explanation is clear to yourself if nobody else.

I thought you were a professional employment agency with substance and ability to add to the whole process of employing people. Obviously I was very wrong, and I do apologize for taking up your time in writing a completely useless and meaningless reply.

Sincerely yours,

Frederick

● ● ●

Dear Mr. Reed,

Thank you for your long email reply detailing your perception of my lack of experience. Unfortunately, you do not recognize talent.

PeopleSoft Management could use your own advice and have much better luck and better responses from recruiting if they just "cut the recruiter out of the loop" and developed their own recruiting department.

I speak with many CEOs, CFOs, Business and Political Leaders regularly, and will now make reference to your firm as a company that works against the potential employee and management. I believe you when you say recruiting fees are problematic for a company to invest in because of the quality of work that you do.

Unfortunately, the PeopleSoft job market tightens because of bad management that you most likely put into place.

The good news is that PeopleSoft will continue to reduce jobs and your company will be partly responsible for it.

I wish you the best of luck as you try to move into the next millennium. Over time, perhaps computers and other quality recruiters will replace your jobs.

Sincerely,

Mary McKinney

• • •

"The misuse of the word 'architect' is punishable under the law"

Please note that you are violating the laws of the Commonwealth of Massachusetts by using the job title "Architect" for a position other than a designer of the construction of buildings. Under the laws of the Commonwealth, an Architect must have at least five years of architectural education, a Bachelor's Degree in Architecture, and must have passed the licensing exam conducted by the Commonwealth. The misuse of the word architect is specifically against the law and is punishable under the law.

You are also, of course, insulting Architects by implying that people who program computers are Architects.

We would appreciate your compliance with the law and changing your practice so that it is not insulting.

(Authors' note: On March 16, 2004, we logged onto Monster.com and searched for Information Technology jobs that contained the keyword "architect." Results? 1803 jobs posted in the last 60 days.)

• • •

We conclude this section with a bit of "back and forth" between Rachel and a job seeker who duked it out, but later came to an understanding, thus proving that a bit of witty repartee can sometimes go where "an eye for an eye" cannot. The interaction kicked off with an email from Rachel responding to a resume submittal:

Dear Jose,

Thank you for applying for the data warehousing job openings on our web site. Unfortunately, while your technical skills are impressive on the DBA level, you do not have the background in business intelligence that is needed for these data warehousing positions. I'm sorry I wasn't able to submit your resumes for these jobs - frankly, I'm not qualified to assess the scope of your skills beyond the data warehousing area, but I'm sure there are some solid openings out there that will be a fit for you. I wish you luck in your search for a new position.

Sincerely,

Rachel Meyers

Mi querida Rachel:

Actually the "sorry" person is not me at all. I am quite optimistic about my chances. Thanks anyway for your "marvelous" feedback. You are qualified, so that is a poor cop out.

p.s. the check for a nickel is in the mail.

Hasta Luego,

Jose

Jose, what are you so annoyed about? I never said or implied that you should not be optimistic about your job search. I simply stated that my specialty is data warehousing. That's the area I consult in. Not to mention that I believe I am in a better position to determine my qualifications than you. Second, I receive literally hundreds of email messages from all over the world from people *in data warehousing* each day. It is simply not possible for me to customize a resume feedback system for each and every individual. And that's for people *in my field.* There's not enough time in the day. I'm sorry if my need to make a living offends you or otherwise impedes your job search. There's no need to be rude.

You want advice? I'll give you some advice: your resume looks great. What you need to work on is your ability to have professional exchanges with those who you are seeking advice from, partnering with, interviewing with, etc.

It's a smaller world than you obviously think. Be careful who you offend.

Rachel

p.s. Let's do lunch!

Estimada Rachel:

You're right. I sounded like a 95 year old man. I apologize for my previous remarks. You are the first person who caused me to open up (Don't know why). Normally, I am quite professional, and formal in all of my emails to your type of companies. Oh well, there's always a first, right? (smile)

I am originally from Boston (a true "Southie." Yes, I survived). Sounds to me that we could have been neighbors at one time. Pure guess. Your sense of humor is quite similar to mine. Well, I know that you are busy but whenever you have to come to Minneapolis, I am open for lunch, brunch, anything you want to call it.

Either way, put me on your "all types of jokes list", you have my permission (if you do send jokes or strange emails at all).

Tu Nuevo Amigo,

Jose

• • •

22
Resume Haters

Some people resent the resume enough to openly question its purpose. We can't fault their objections, but we do wonder if the resume itself is the best vehicle for the expression of such.

• • •

You should note that, despite my best efforts, there seems to be something lacking in my resume. Perhaps this is because I was raised in northern Maine, whose people value reticence and understatement, and have no facility for the hyperbole and self aggrandizement that seems to be the hallmark of all good resumes, or at least those given as examples in the 'resume handbooks' I have been reading. But I suspect that my difficulty resides on another level, that of description. After 20 years in the computer industry, I have yet to find a satisfactory explanation of what I do.

• • •

Dear Jon, Rachel, & Associates

I don't know if you'll obtain this letter, but I propose my candidature for your corporation as good mimicry (adaptive) computer (program) specialist. What does it mean?

My current qualification means nothing.

Here's also my resume but it also MEANS NOTHING...

• • •

Please note that the attached resume is a true and accurate educational and employment history dating back to 1964, however, does not project a true image of my overall skills, interests, or production quality with respect to positions with a computer orientation.

• • •

23
Buyer Beware

We all have at least one secret that would raise the eyebrows of a prospective employer. But since we don't bother to divulge that information, we get hired, everyone gets paid, and life goes on. Not so for Mr. and Mrs. "Buyer Beware." These folks take a confessional approach to resume writing, unintentionally raising questions about their own integrity and workplace ethics. Perhaps their hope is that total honesty will lead to total respect. But the world is a complicated place, and confessions usually come with a price tag.

• • •

Relocation information: Willing to relocate.

Contracts or perm: Would want to work in a consulting firm.

Amount of travel: Moderate.

Additional Comments: I recently signed an agreement with Unitech back in the UK that I'll work with them for 2 years. However, I'll not be respecting this agreement when I get a better offer.

• • •

Amount of Travel: moderate

Additional Comments: Lawson Technical Team Lead

Availability: 1-2 months after accepting offer.

• • •

Employment

10/1996 to Present   Access Tech   US-AR-Little Rock

SQL*Server and Oracle Database Designer

Education

1/1994   Bingham University   US-VA-Richmond

Bachelors of Science Degree in Applied Mathematics

Additional Information

Most employers say that I am a very ethical employee.

• • •

24
Job Orders from Hell:
Recruiters Gone Wild

It's not just job seekers who have entertained us over the years. Sometimes we get our entertainment from the other side of the negotiating table. From ethnic slurs to bad puns, our fellow recruiters have the bases covered. Not all of the bad stuff is funny - heck, some of it isn't even printable. But just as with resumes, much of what makes a job order funny involves a violation of formality - an unsolicited opinion here, a bit of political commentary there. That's why most of the jobs in the section are not from corporate HR departments, but from informal recruiter-to-recruiter correspondence. Perhaps the assumption is that you can relax around your friends. But is every recipient in your "email job blast" your buddy? And is it a good idea to kick off a business partnership with a job order that is just one step ahead of anti-discrimination statutes? We're not sure, but opinionated rants can sure spice up a job order. As with all the sections in this book, any typos and grammatical flaws you see are all part of the fun.

• • •

IT programming positions, huge team, no management opportunities, no opportunity for advancement. Need folks with lesser ambition who are content with repetitive work: WORKER BEES ONLY!

• • •

Looking for Action

Fee: Flat rate $4,000 - We do very little work, they have a three step interview and they handle all the setup of those and I bird dog them.

Good company has doubled its size every year since 1990. They call when they need help.

We feel paper sitting in a file drawer is not making money, but people we are actively working will never know this company exists. We have told them that also and they understand.

• • •

A common tendency among recruiters is to make jobs sound cooler than they really are. This recruiter did his best to inject some street credibility into a typical Monday-through-Friday "road warrior" consulting job with one of the largest consultancies in the world. Incidentally, the firm was going through a major restructuring at the time the job order was written - hardly a sexy time to get on board. Anyone who fell for this job was likely part of the mass layoffs that occurred six months later.

Job Title: Software Implementation Freak

This progressive company wants you to help them duke it out with the best… and be a winner. The boys & girls of summer need additional players who want to help them make things happen for some of the world's top companies. If you have a desire to play in the sand and sweat bullets, then don't be afraid to take a look at our client's cool job opportunity. This may change your life! Assist in how a firm re-designs its game plan. Work with clients who are serious about changing and who will go to extreme measures to do so. Execute business processes that get results, not the paper shredder.

If you have a desire to play in the sand and sweat bullets...

Job Title: Software Engineer

The hiring manager used the word "despirate" in talking about his staffing situation.

• • •

Job Title: Paradox Programmer

Paradox experience not required.

The logic behind not requiring Paradox is that a good programmer is programming in one of the other packages, not Paradox.

• • •

To my fellow headhunters:

Happy Huntin'!

Scarborough firm with 10-year buddy could hire BRIGHT $25K-$40K kids with CLEAN RECORD and company will go for TS/EBI. "Real Spooks" needed.

Also, just returned from Hartford area visiting clients. 17-year buddy with 509 Department of Defense jobs. Will NOT hire used/ancient trash or Turkeys.

Call/email if you have any sparklers. Still looking for tons. Can send specific attractive job descriptions, if you want to work. Ever try molasses -- still around.

• • •

Job Order Title: Many Programmers Needed, Many Cubicles to Fill

• • •

Jobs that suffer from an excess of formality and detail can be equally entertaining:

The normal work environment is typical of a business office, manufacturing cleanroom, applications laboratory, and support areas such as stockroom and machine shop.

The incumbent may occasionally lift or move up to 35 pounds.

While performing the regular duties of the position, the incumbent may be exposed to moving mechanical parts, risk of electric shock, and possible exposure to toxic or caustic chemicals.

The incumbent is routinely required to sit, stand, walk, touch, see, and hear.

• • •

More highlights from recruiter-to-recruiter "email blasts":

Hi: spent 'til 3am putting this together (didn't realize past my cradle time). I had a great time doing it. I am proud AS YOU ARE to present candidates with exact qualifications. Hopefully, you can send one or two on-target candidates. Please don't clean up your desk and send me old paper for which you expect a check @35% on $142,740, which, according to my Abacus, comes to a $49,559 fee. We both have to do some work to get the fee. They almost seems like the new monopoly $100s - but the checks are for real.

• • •

Hot Reqs from The Defense Sector

Have some great positions in the Defense industry for the sharpest shooting technical minds out there. Make sure you find out what they can do for us and when will they be able to start...

"You know the rest of the story."

We need to find the best!

(If you remember, the PATRIOT missile MISSED most of the targets. I don't believe they want to have the same experience. Also, if you remember, one of the ships in the Persian Gulf ages before, misidentified a plane as it wasn't on the RADAR screen. Commander had 7 minutes to identify friend/foe. Thought it was a foe, so 200 people dead).

Editorial comment by me as taxpayer but makes common sense with cooler heads.

So SEND THE BEST and TOSS THE REST!

• • •

BIG BANK BOOM '96!

Help me make placements in '96 with the Worldwide Market Leader... details below.

My sister-in-law died March 4, 1995, capping off 57 year old wife dying six years ago and Mensa brother dying recently, so only leaves me for the wooden box. But he hasn't measured mine yet!

Anyway, here's what I'm looking for now....

• • •

When I told an HR rep about full contents needed in the interview pre-package, I told her she forgot one item. On quizzing me, mentioned to her: Although the offer letter was just a formality, they could save an increase in the postage for a later separate offer letter and it would have two benefits:

1. As a taxpayer it would cut down on my taxes by using the same pre-package for inclusion of the offer letter in that first package. Savings: .28 cents.

2. The candidate would feel much more at ease during the interview if he already had the offer.

• • •

25
Pardon My Racism

We all have some prejudice in our little brains. Some of us are working on ridding ourselves of it, some of us are trying to hide it, and some of us slip it onto our resumes. Fortunately, most folks seem to have the good sense to steer clear of anything that might appear to be an ethnic slight. But as always, there are a couple of envelope-pushers out there.

• • •

74-77 HUMANITIES: (SERVE AMERICA) 9 mo-Black Ghetto (food & empl), 5 mo-rural Anglos (motivation), 8 mo-Chicano (work ethics), 10 mo-families (counseling), 2 mo-elderly (interpersonal relations), 12 mo-(suicide). I gave a lot and learned even more.

• • •

City of Northern Wind, China: I provided new ideas and plans to attract business to this no-where land. Today it is a booming business mecca.

• • •

We also hear from those who are free from bias:

Ladies and Gentlemen:

I appreciate very much the opportunity to apply for the position of Business Analyst in your organization and to inform you more about me.

I have excellent interpersonal skills and manners. I treat all people with respect. I have absolutely no prejudices.

Thank you,

Jerry Logan

• • •

26
Odd Jobs and Telling Titles

Some people have funky ways of describing ordinary jobs; others have truly funky jobs. Check out some of the odder jobs we've seen over the years.

• • •

Human Resources Director

Jacksonville Savings and Trust, Jacksonville, FL

Develop and oversee all areas of a non-existing human resources department.

• • •

I invented more successful diets than any other person in the world.

• • •

Crashed trains into mannequin filled automobiles for safety research.

• • •

Quality Caskets, Inc.: Retail store for casket and accessory hardware for the interment of human remains.

• • •

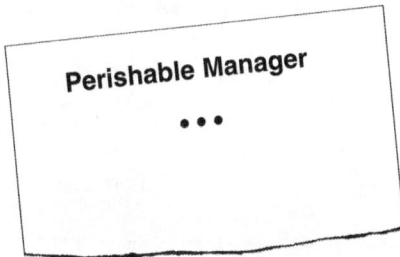

Perishable Manager

• • •

This person was applying for a Visual C++ programming job:

I was the world's NUMBER ONE fanny pack designer who created today's fanny pack industry.

• • •

27
Let Me Impress You With
My Little Black Book

"It's not how hard you work, but who you know." Isn't that the truth? How many times have we missed out on opportunities because we were just too many "degrees of Kevin Bacon" away from Donald Trump? The folks below offer some reassurances on that subject. For all their social connections, they're still shopping their resume around, same as you and me. Maybe it doesn't come down to who you know after all - or maybe knowing Lyle Alzado just doesn't have the same pull as it used to.

• • •

Gentlepersons:

I'd like to try to impress you with my family's prominence. My father was an elected official for ten years on the Baltimore School Board and served three years as President. He was in the Chief of Staff's Office in Baltimore under Clarence Bishop, and when Martin O'Malley came in as Mayor, he appointed my father as Education Commissioner. My sister, a lawyer, was Vice-President Gore's Assistant Chief of Staff in the White House and when Clinton was re-elected President, she became Chairman of the Working People, Working Wages Campaign.

You will never find a better or more dedicated worker. I work hard, love computers, and am an excellent programmer. I have an I.Q. of 149.

Sincerely yours,

Steve Robinson, Jr.

• • •

It is a FACT that almost every BILLIONAIRE in the world attended my parties. I created and owned the very private club, Debonairres and Damsels, in New York City. Men were required to have a personal net worth over $250 MILLION to join. And women only had to be extremely beautiful and pay me a negotiable fee.

• • •

Presently, I have very good personal/business contacts in both Shanghai (a nano-technology Scientist and his wife, an active Violinist) and New Delhi (a Telecommunications Technology Guru).

• • •

I was solely responsible for personally hiring and negotiating all contracts for hundreds of famous celebrities and NOT their agents! Negotiated directly with hundreds of celebrities including: Gary Busey, Clint Eastwood, Bill Bixby, Loni Anderson, Larry Hagman, Mickey Rooney, Chevy Chase, Valerie Bertinelli, Loretta Swit, Tony Danza, Joe Piscopo, Alan Alda, Steve Allen, Linda Gray, Tony Curtis, Parker Stevenson, Margaux Hemingway, Sally Struthers, James Brolin, Lyle Alzado, Vincent Price, etc.

• • •

I personally know many of the presidents and military leaders of countries in Sub-Saharan Africa, as well as the wealthiest families in Puerto Rico and the Caribbean Islands.

• • •

28
When Words Won't Do:
Graphics from Hell

The best resume graphics provide a visual structure for data that directly relates to work experience, such as a chart of relevant technical skills. But when a resume gets a little more visually adventurous, we're heading into deeper waters. For example, trying to portray how all your personal time is spent - including weekends - in the form of a bar graph, is an ill-advised undertaking. Using a grid to track one's life back to grade school is another questionable pursuit. When it comes to resume graphics, ambition can truly be a detriment, as is demonstrated by the executive who tried to separate out and then re-integrate all aspects of his skills into a flow chart. This Captain Ahab of the resume graphics world ignored all ports of call and headed out to high sea. Let's take a look at some of the resume graphics that have made an impression on us.

• • •

Aren't graphs supposed to make things clearer?

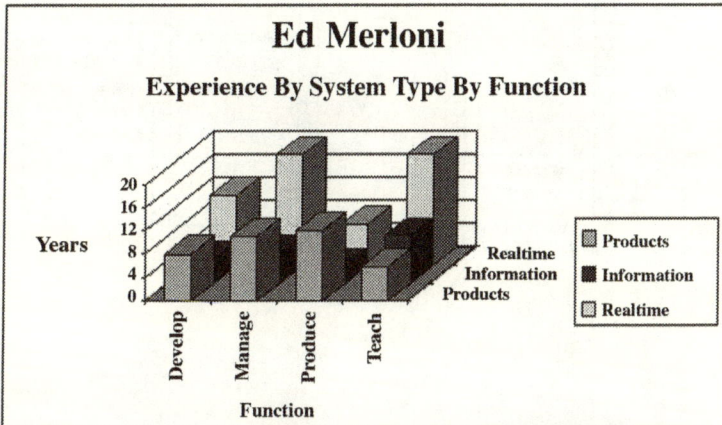

Ed Merloni

Experience By System Type By Function

Years — 20 16 12 8 4 0

Realtime / Information / Products

Function: Develop / Manage / Produce / Teach

Products / Information / Realtime

• • •

We were wondering, what's so great about Tuesdays?

	LTI (high school)			
1987		chairman of VCOMM		
1988	tue	secretary of VCOMM		
1989		treasurer of VMAC	editor-in-chief of LSPG Quarterly	
1990	Florida University of Technology			FCT work for the Off-site Learning Center of the University
1991				
1992		operator & consultant at the Tutoring Initiative		
1993				
1994			sales assistant at Banana Republic	Senior Research Assistant at RVC Applied Technology (University Affiliate)
1995				
1997	graduation project			

• • •

Here's our "Captain Ahab" who created a total skills integration flow chart:

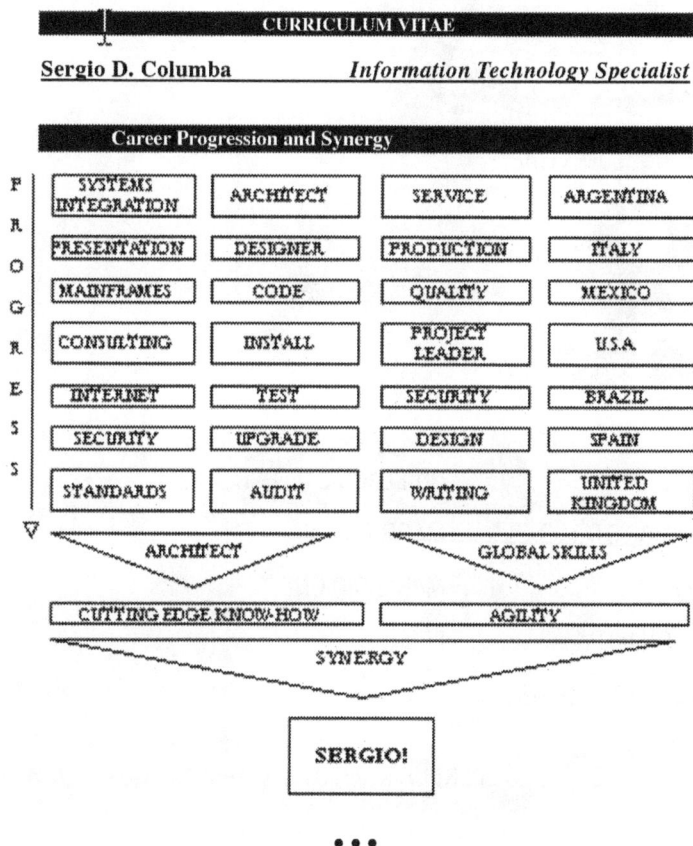

CURRICULUM VITAE			
Sergio D. Columba		*Information Technology Specialist*	

Career Progression and Synergy

P R O G R E S S			
SYSTEMS INTEGRATION	ARCHITECT	SERVICE	ARGENTINA
PRESENTATION	DESIGNER	PRODUCTION	ITALY
MAINFRAMES	CODE	QUALITY	MEXICO
CONSULTING	INSTALL	PROJECT LEADER	U.S.A.
INTERNET	TEST	SECURITY	BRAZIL
SECURITY	UPGRADE	DESIGN	SPAIN
STANDARDS	AUDIT	WRITING	UNITED KINGDOM

ARCHITECT   GLOBAL SKILLS

CUTTING EDGE KNOW-HOW   AGILITY

SYNERGY

SERGIO!

• • •

And here's someone who got a little carried away with clip art:

CURRICULUM VITAE

1. PERSONAL

NAME	GUILLAUME C LEONE
MARITAL STATUS	MARRIED
WIFE	MARIE CICIONE
NATIONALITY	FRENCH

2. ACADEMIC DEGREES

INFORMATION TECHNOLOGY	BERLIN INSTITUTE OF TECHNOLOGY
LANGUAGES	ENGLISH, SPANISH 85% READING, WRITING, CONVERSATION

READING, WRITING, CONVERSATION
GERMAN, BASIC 30%

PROFESSIONAL EXPERIENCE

1983-1988   PRODUCER OF ALCOHOLIC BEVERAGES

BREWERY MANAGER:
SUPERVISE PRODUCTION PROCESS

PRODUCTION CONTROL AND MAINTENANCE:
DESIGNER OF TWO NEW PRODUCTION LINES

1980-1982   PRODUCER OF ALCOHOLIC BEVERAGES

PRODUCTION MANAGER -
QUALITY CONTROL: MONITOR PURITY AND BEVERAGE QUALITY

INSTALLATION OF NEW SELF-TIMED BEVERAGE
PRODUCTION LINE

1975-1980   TELEFONE DE FRANCE.

CHIEF OF TELECOMM RESEARCH AND ENGINEERING
PLANNED ADDITIONAL DOWNLINE GROWTH MODEL

DIRECTOR OF ENGINEERING:
PLAN AND PREPARE FOR THE DEPLOYMENT OF NEW VOICE
TRANSMISSION LINES

==========

EXTRA ACTIVITIES

AT THE UNIVERSITY   PRESIDENT OF STUDENTS SOCIETY OF
INFORMATION TECHNOLOGY 1973-1976
FOOTBALL PLAYER ON THE UNIVERSITY TEAM

OUT OF THE UNIVERSITY

SHOTOKAN KARATE SINCE FIFTH GRADE

MEMBER OF U.S. PROJECT MANAGER'S INSTITUTE
SCIENCE TEACHER

------ ---- ---- ---

<u>HOBBIES</u>

outdoor sports like:

Fishing, skiing, hunting

Miniature Woodcarving and Glass Burning

• • •

29
Maybe You *Should* Quit Your Day Job

Now that we've filled an entire book with cautionary examples of overly creative and personalized resumes, it's time for a confession: there are a few folks out there who can make us laugh and score the interview at the same time. Their efforts are defiant proof that resumes can get some laughs without doing a belly flop.

• • •

This chap found a funny and appealing way to account for a stretch of unemployment:

David Colantonio

Aug 1996 - Jan 1997

Dave's House (well-earned vacation)

Couch Potato/Housekeeper

Duties included sitting/sleeping on futon, watching "Twilight Zone" re-runs. Also sat through many episodes of "The Dukes of Hazzard," and many first-run movies on cable. Was primarily tasked with maintaining a tidy living area, including kitchen and bathroom. Technology utilized included power vacuum equipment, automatic dishwasher, and some manual tools. Was directly responsible for consulting 3 boxes of Charleston Chews and 1 case of Coke per week. Stood and looked at the NordicTrack for hours on end.

• • •

When you take this kind of approach, you have to hope that the hiring manager has a sense of humor:

Subject: Job #03587CC... Looking for Mr. Right Company...

SWF - 33, 5'7" blue eyes, brown hair, with excessive amounts of energy, seeking lots of creative times with the right company. I am not looking for a long term commitment on the first date, but I would like to explore the possibility of developing a special relationship which will be mutually satisfying. I am very experienced. I have been doing my thing for 12 years and I love every minute of it. Why don't you stop by my home page for a little interactivity? Don't be shy. Reach out and touch my on-line resume, portfolio, and bio. Keep the light on, you'll want to watch the animated image, my typography and electronic illustrations.

• • •

Here's a self-questionnaire approach that worked - primarily because it was geared toward addressing the specific skills we were hiring for. We're not sure what this person meant by "agile," but he charmed us nonetheless:

Hi!

1. Are you looking for hiring a Materials Management consultant?

2. Should he be PeopleSoft certified?

3. Should he have around 2 years of PS exposure?

4. Should he have PS implementation experience in Telecom, engineering & automotive industry?

5. Should he be working on the 4.3 release of PeopleSoft?

6. Should he be bright, outgoing and agile?

If your answer to all the above is "Yes", then you need to hire PeopleSoft professional Anil Srinivasan !!!!!!!

• • •

It's hard to make descriptions of technical work come to life. This person pulled it off:

A Query System for Automated Motorcycle Dealer. The automated motorcycle dealer prototype system is designed to permit a user to order a motorcycle by computer via a modem. He types his request for a motorcycle in common English paragraph (not a simple order entry form), specifies the make, model, and type of payments. For instance, 'Hello, my name is Ben. I would like a Yamaha motorcycle. Did you get that? I want the turbo option. Can I have it in red?' The automated invoice taker will take an invoice with customer name Ben, and a red, turbo Yamaha motorcycle.

• • •

Although it's hard to come up with a viable resume when you have no work history or education, we have to admire the spunk of this sixteen year old:

Work History

"unknown at this time"

Education

"currently in between grades"

• • •

This job seeker charmed/hypnotized us with a subliminal message underneath his job description:

Summary: Technical explanation… I am a seasoned C++ programmer who has developed and designed numerous C++ extensions and applications. I have worked with classes, exceptions, and event-driven programming. I also have experience designing multi-server databases using macros, menus, toolbars, forms, queries, and reports.

Hire me • Hire me • Hire me • Hire me • Hire me • Hire me • Hire me • Hire me • Hire me • Hire me • Hire me • Hire me • Hire me • Hire me • Hire me • Hire me •

• • •

Meet the Authors

About Jon Reed: Jon wrote his first resume when he was seventeen years old. It was not good. Since then, he has dedicated himself to improving his resume through a two-prong strategy: acquiring new work experiences and listing them in chronological order. Jon's career includes a series of misadventures in publishing, recruiting, project management, and web site development. Jon has been involved in some hiring and some firing over the years, and has seen his fair share of resumes. His only regret about this book is that the best resume of all, which linked various projects with corresponding episodes of "Star Trek," could not be printed for copyright reasons. Those readers who dare to venture further into Jon's writing on pop culture and other obsessions are invited to check out www.jonreed.net. Jon's email is jon@resumes fromhell.com.

About Rachel Meyers: Rachel's professional history includes, in no particular order: recruiter, ice cream scooper, legal secretary, pharmaceutical conference producer, police department administrator, web site developer, Jon Reed's editor, and Friendly's® waitress. Her (ir)relevant educational qualifications are a Bachelors of Corrections in Criminal Justice and Dolphin School. If she were inclined to list hobbies and pastimes on her resume, they would include martial arts, belly dancing, traveling to warm and exotic places, and finding ways to tread more lightly upon this Earth. Email Rachel about any of these subjects at rachel@resumes fromhell.com.

Meet The Illustrator

About Rusty Johnson: Rusty and Jon Reed have known each other since 1980 when they were matched in the Big Brother/Little Brother program of Tulsa, Oklahoma (Rusty was the Big Brother). Rusty is a university degreed "commercial artist," but his favored work was in the cartooning area, until six years ago, when he seriously embraced woodcarving. When one of his co-workers suggested that his woodcarving looked like his cartooning, he felt that he had achieved artistic "oneness." Rusty can be reached via email at rusty@resumesfromhell.com if you want to talk about cartoons, both two- and three-dimensional, or view his award-winning carvings. And yes, most of his carved figures have only three fingers.

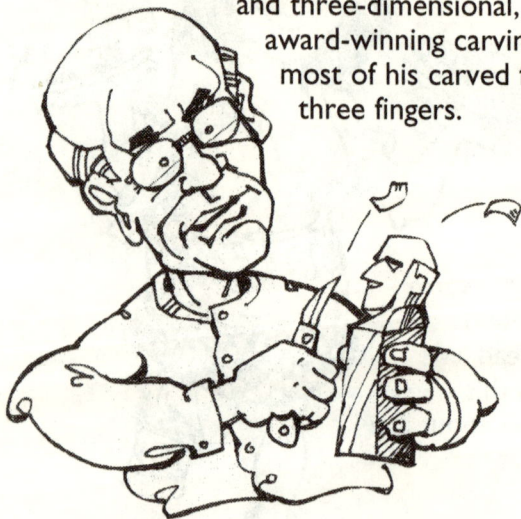

Resumes from Hell – Book Index

www.ingramcontent.com/pod-product-compliance
Lightning Source LLC
Chambersburg PA
CBHW022111210326
41521CB00028B/269